Good Services

Services

Lou Downe

To the designers in the UK government, whose commitment to building better services has meant that this book was an idea in the first place.

To my wife Sarah, without whom this book would be just another idea on my ever-growing list.

And to Mum and Dad, whose unwavering support has meant it's been possible for me to have ideas that turn into books.

Good Services

How to design services that work

Lou Downe

Foreword
Mike Monteiro

There used to be a tree in front of our house. It was, by the entire neighbourhood's admission, a very ugly tree. It had greyish bark, sticky sickly looking leaves, a generally unpleasing shape, and didn't appear to be in the best of health. But it was our tree. It blocked the afternoon sun from our living room, and our dog liked to pee on it. We were glad to have it.

Then a large branch fell. A thick, heavy branch. Right onto a neighbour's car. Luckily, no one got hurt. The neighbour's car was a little dented, which he wasn't happy about but, all in all, it could've been a lot worse. Life went back to normal. People went back to parking under the tree, and dogs went back to peeing on it. Until a few weeks later there was a heavy wind and another branch came down. The tree's time had come. A city worker came by and taped a notice to the tree, alerting us that it was marked for removal. I wasn't happy to lose the tree, but it was obvious the tree was now dangerous and had to go. Luckily, the notice contained a URL where I could go to ask the city for a new tree.

This is where our story takes a dark turn.

Years of dealing with local government services websites have taught me a few things. First, make sure you are alone, because you are going to get angry. Second, have your anxiety medication nearby. Carve out at least half a day. Make sure the dog's water bowl is full. Update your will. And alert your neighbours to ignore the screams. If they look worried, just tell them you're using a local government website. Watch as their concern turns to pity. Some of them may offer to bring you meals.

Sadly, all that preparation was in vain, because the first thing I found out on the new tree website was that, before I could get a new tree, I had to request a stump removal. Which was handled by a different department, on a different website. Also, I didn't have a stump yet. I still had an ugly yet beloved tree. I had to wait until I had a stump.

Two weeks later, workers came, cut down the tree and left a stump. I had my prerequisite for getting a new tree. I went to the stump removal website, and asked them to remove my stump. A week later, they did. Which meant that I could now go to the new tree website to request a new tree. First question: is this a replacement tree? Easy enough. Has the stump been removed? Oh, yes! So much progress. Third question: what kind of tree do you want? Reader, there was a drop-down list. I clicked.

Let's take a nature break. Do you know how many types of trees there are? There are a lot. There are deciduous trees, which lose their leaves with the seasons, and evergreen trees, which do not. In addition there are palm trees, banana trees and, oddly, bamboo is a tree. I didn't know that. But I do now. Because it was listed in that drop-down list. Along with every other tree on earth. They were all in the list. Including sequoias. Now, I'm the kind of jerk that if someone is willing to plant a sequoia in front of my house, I'll take it. So I said, yes, give me a sequoia.

A week later I got an email that said, no, you cannot have a sequoia. It's not the right kind of tree for your neighbourhood. Ok, well, I guess that's on me. I knew I was being a jerk when I selected it. But it's also on you, for having it on the list. Regardless, I probably knew I shouldn't have asked for a sequoia. I went back to the list. I picked something else, I think it was an oak tree, because that sounded like a non-jerk choice. A week later: no, you cannot have an oak. I tried again. Cypress? (Possibly because I was listening to Cypress Hill.) Again, no. Wrong tree. Why couldn't the city just tell me what kind of tree I *could* have? This went on for a while, until one day I came home to find the city had cemented over the whole thing, and some kid had written LORD SALAMANDER in the wet cement.

I never got a tree.

In this particular case, as much as I enjoyed my ugly tree, it wasn't a catastrophic loss. It was annoying. But the same city that runs that online service also runs services for starting small businesses, getting married, jury duty, the municipal courts and law enforcement. And I guarantee you those are designed just as well. And that's just the city stuff.

Every day, all over the world, people go online to accomplish things. They're signing up for stuff. They're checking their finances. They're getting tickets to something. They're making medical appointments and, if they're in the US, they're checking to see whether their insurance company covers a procedure they need. They're checking on their citizenship application status. They're applying to schools and trying to see if they qualify for a loan so they can afford it.

For the most part, no one wants to be doing these things. They're not exciting. They're tolls for existence. We want to get through them as quickly as possible so we can get back to the stuff we actually want to do. Sadly, using these services too often turns into a frustrating experience. Made all the more frustrating because you didn't want to be doing it anyway.

Here's where we come in. If you're reading this book, it's probably because you have something to do with designing services of one sort or another. And I'm gonna go out on a limb and assume that you're the type of person who cares about doing this right, because, duh, you're reading a book about it. And you're looking for help in doing the right thing. Well, I have good news for you. This book is going to help. I've read it! It's well-written. It's helpful. And it's brilliant. And it's written to help you help other do what they need.

Lou Downe has been designing good services for quite a while. And they're good at it! I can't tell you how many times I got stuck trying to solve something and thought: 'Well, let's go see how GOV.UK solved it.' I have no doubt that Lou is a good designer, because I've stolen their work more than once. But as much as Lou cares about design, I think they care about people even more. And that's the secret. You've got to care more about the people on the other end of the screen than about what's on the screen. You've got to help them get on with their day. So they can do the stuff that really matters to them.

Some people say that good design is invisible. That when it's done right you shouldn't notice it. I say they're looking in the wrong place. Turn around. Good design is very visible. It's visible on the face of every person who's ever used a well-designed service. The slightly raised eyebrow that says, 'huh, I expected that to be a lot harder', followed by a recognition that they just reclaimed some time to read a book, or play with their kid, or walk their dog – whatever it is they actually want to do. That's good design. It's pretty visible. You just need to know where to look.

We don't design for screens. We don't design for organisations. We don't design for shareholders. We design for people.

I have no doubt that if Lou Downe had overseen the design of that local government website, I'd have a tree right now.

Foreword
Marc Stickdorn

Think about all of the different services that you experienced today. Did you check your bank balance on the way to work? Get on a bus? Buy this book from your local bookshop?

Think about the different parts of the services you experienced – the different channels you've used, and the different parts of an organisation you came in to contact with, without even knowing it.

Now, think about who was responsible for creating the different parts of those services: the managers, software developers, marketers, sales representatives, customer support officers, lawyers, engineers, architects, accountants and, of course, designers.

Think about how many of those people are working on changes that might have an effect on the service you've just used – the infrastructure building projects, changes to internal software, accounting processes or legal terms and conditions.

All of these projects affect the experience that customers, users, employees and citizens have of our services; but how many of these things were designed intentionally, or with a knowledge of how they might affect a user's experience? And how many of these were designed with a knowledge of what a good service looked like?

The reality is: very few.

Users don't care who designed the services they use. They only care if services meet their needs, or at least match their expectations. In short: if they're good.

For many years, we've been discussing what service design is and how it works.

Service design has been taught in design schools and practised since the mid-1990s, at places such as Köln International School of Design (KISD) and the first dedicated service design agencies, such as LiveWork and Engine.

When I was teaching at one of these early service design courses in 2008 (at the MCI business school in Innsbruck, Austria) there were still no textbooks out there on this topic.

Together with Jakob Schneider, we decided to simply write it ourselves. 'This Is Service Design Thinking' was published in 2011 and brought together 23 co-authors from the service design community.

It was intended simply as a textbook to be used by students during courses, but the fact that it later became an international bestseller is testament to the massive growth of service design all over the world.

When I look back at the 10 years since Jakob and I published our book, we've not just seen a huge growth in service design, but also a huge change in the way that it has developed.

More and more education programmes, agencies and in-house teams have adopted service design, and a wave of acquisitions of service design agencies has finally proved how much business now values the activity of consciously designing services.

In less than two decades, we've gone from discussions about how to raise awareness of the fact that services need to be actively designed, to how we scale that activity beyond the boundaries of service designers.

In this new phase of service design, a discussion on what we're aiming for when we design services is long overdue.

'We talk about "what good looks like" in service design... but has anyone actually ever defined it?' Lou tweeted this question on 20 March 2018. This led to numerous discussions, talks and a blog post that was widely shared in and beyond the service design community. Now, less than two years later, you can read what makes good services in this book.

Service design is a team sport – and a definition of good services with common principles gives you and everyone else working on your service a common focus and goal. Here, however, we see competing mindsets: while some push towards adding new 'wow' factors to a service, perhaps to drive marketing and sales, others strive to fix the basics first.

I estimate that 95% of service design projects are about fixing the basics. The principles outlined in this book have the potential to act as a North Star, leading people to create good services and thereby a much better experience for users, customer, employees and citizens. But by establishing a baseline for 'good' services, we can also be much more efficient in the way that we work, and spend more of our time on the things that are unique to our services, rather than the things that aren't.

This is not the first time we've tried to define what we mean by a 'good' service that works for users. In 1977 and 1980, Richard Oliver published the widely known 'Expectation Confirmation Theory'. Summarised simply, it states that customer satisfaction is the result of a comparison of our expectations with our experience. If they match, we're satisfied; if experience prevails expectations, we're delighted; but if expectations outweigh experience, we're dissatisfied. In 1984, Professor Noriaki Kano published the 'Kano Model', a theory for product development and customer satisfaction. It describes three main factors: basic factors ('Must-be Quality') that, similar to hygiene factors, do not contribute to satisfaction but cause dissatisfaction if missing; performance factors ('One-dimensional Quality') that can contribute to dissatisfaction when they're missing, but also to satisfaction when they are implemented well; and excitement factors ('Attractive Quality') that only contribute to satisfaction, but cause dissatisfaction when they're missing.

Did you read the above paragraph? Or did you skip it when you read 'academic literature' and saw sources and academic concepts mentioned in the paragraph?

Often, academic research provides useful answers, but, unfortunately, it is not accessible enough in practice. My hope is that this book serves as a bridge between practical hands-on guidance on how to build a good service, and grounded principles that we can use to guide our industry.

I have no doubt that this book will become a must-read for the service design community, but this book is also for everyone working with services – consciously or unconsciously.

Talking about what makes good services is vital within the service design community, and will help us to further mature our practice, but these principles can help to leverage service design way beyond the service design community.

This book shouldn't be seen as the 'end' of defining what makes good services, but rather as a starting point for a more educated discussion on this topic.

As Professor Richard Buchanan said in 2001: 'One of the great strengths of design is that we have not settled on a single definition. Fields in which definition is now a settled matter tend to be lethargic, dying, or dead fields, where inquiry no longer provides challenges to what is accepted as truth.' Thus, this book shouldn't be seen as the 'end' of defining what makes good services, but rather as a starting point for a more educated discussion on this topic. It is a milestone defining how we see what makes good services now. This will change and evolve but, once we have a point of reference, we can build on this milestone and use it as a springboard to design better services and, over time, improve the principles and definitions of a good service.

Wha
serv

t is a
ice?

This is a book about good services – what they are and how to design them.

It will tell you what a good service looks like, and what a bad one looks like too. It will give you advice on how to design, build and run services that work for your users, but before we can get to that, we must first define what we mean by a 'service'.

Services are everywhere. From how we book our holidays, to how we save money and get access to healthcare. Ask someone on the street what a service is, however, or what it means to design one, and they will probably struggle to tell you.

For something so ubiquitous and fundamental to how we live our lives, it might seem strange that services are so rarely thought about, and so often misunderstood. Yet services exist in the background by their very nature. They are the things that connect other things, the spaces between things – such as choosing a new car and having it delivered or booking an appointment at your GP and being successfully treated. We barely notice them until we encounter something that stands out as good or bad.

For the organisations that provide them, services are often barely more visible than they are for users. They require multiple people, and sometimes multiple organisations to provide all of the steps that a user needs to complete to achieve their goal. Sometimes there are so many pieces to this puzzle, or it stretches across such a long period of time that we struggle to see them as a whole.

And yet it's services that are the interface to so much of our experience of the world. From having children, getting married, moving house and, ultimately, death, services facilitate some of the most important moments in our lives.

To understand what it means to design a good service, we must understand the definition of 'service'.

There are much longer books than this one that have explained what services are in minute detail and, although a lot of those definitions are accurate, most are long, complicated and almost impossible to remember, let alone apply to the real world. What's even more troubling about these definitions is that they often claim that services are 'intangible', making them sound almost as if they are too complex or nebulous to be designed.

But services aren't complicated, and they don't deserve the complicated explanations they've been given in the past.

A service is something that helps someone to do something

A service, simply put, is simply something that helps someone to do something. That 'something' can be short and straightforward, like buying a chocolate bar, or it can be long and in multiple parts, like moving house. What unites all services is that they help us to achieve a goal, however big or small it might be. The parts of a service might be provided by a number of different organisations but, to a user, a service is one continuous set of actions towards that end goal, regardless of who is providing it.

Services are often hugely affected by the channel in which they're designed to be provided, and you can chart their evolution over time by the rise and fall of the technologies we use to access them. It's therefore important to know a little bit about the history and evolution of services in order to understand how to design a good one for the world we live in now.

A (very) brief history of services

If services are things that help people to do things, then services have existed for as long as people have helped each other to do things.

Homeowners on byways have helped people to sleep safely on long journeys way before we had 'hotels', and certain religious organisations 'looked after' people's money before anyone coined the term 'banking'.

Services can be thought of in conjunction with 'products' – with the service being the things that exist around this product. For example, the service isn't the hotel itself or the money in a bank, it's the process of booking a hotel room, of opening a bank account or making a complaint.

How we access these things is affected by the technology we use at the time. Opening a bank account in the 1900s by written correspondence was very different than it is now, when the same function can be done through an app on your phone.

Above all other changes in technology and culture as we know it, there are three things that have influenced our understanding of services more than anything else: the invention of the postal service, the telephone and the internet.

With the invention of the postal service, and with the growth of the newspapers, magazines and printed advertising that went along with it, we were suddenly able to access services remotely where we would have previously had to access the service in person.

Almost overnight we were able to send away for something in a newspaper, or write to a hotel to book it in advance, instead of visiting a physical location to access that service.

Our choice of service at this time was largely dictated by how well the marketing of that service worked, given that we weren't able to do any research on a service before using it, unless a friend or family member had used it before.

Multibillion dollar business Sears is a perfect example of this era, launching its mail order catalogue in 1906 in a format that was smaller than any magazine, just so it would be placed at the top of any coffee table reading pile.

With the invention of the postal service, suddenly the thing we were trying to do was separate to the service of getting access to it in a way that it had never been before, and telephony furthered this still – now you could not only get access to products and issue direct instructions remotely, but make enquiries, ask questions and make complaints, all from the comfort of your own home (or phone box!).

Now that more people were involved with providing services, those services needed to be standardised in a way that they could be provided consistently. The dawn of computerisation in the 1960s saw an upswell in standardised processes, forms and algorithmic decision-making that was to continue for another 30 years, until the invention of the internet as we know it.

With the invention of the internet, the product and the service became the same thing once again, as the process of signing up, signing in and using the service all became part of one continuous journey. The direct connection between thinking about using a service and actually using it had been re-established – in a way it hadn't been since simply rocking up to an inn and asking to sleep. So services were once more judged on functionality or the usefulness they could bring to our lives through trial and error, not simply the power of the marketing message.

Advertising was no longer able to sell us something that we couldn't prove worked, or wasn't useful in the same way that it

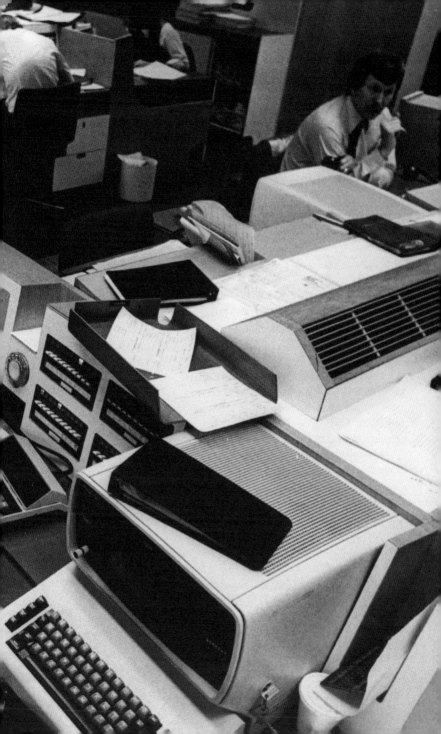

once did, and we now exist in a world where we compete on the quality of our services, not the strength of our messages.

But the transition from one method of delivery to another hasn't always been plain sailing. Services are so affected by the technology we use to deliver them, that they often retain the ways of working that this technology dictates, well after they have been moved to another channel, unless great effort has been taken to understand how that service should work in its new incarnation.

When the internet happened, the majority of these pre-internet services were 'digitised' in order to be consumed through 21st-century channels, but otherwise remained mostly unchanged.

For organisations that predate the internet, this has often meant operating a portfolio of services of differing vintages, each bearing the hallmarks of the era in which they were designed and that, ultimately, don't work in the way that services native to the internet do.

These services were designed for a world where a person was always on hand to help you to do something – be that filling in a form, choosing a product or returning something. But this is not how services work on the internet. Services that needed expert knowledge were fine in the 1920s when we experts were on hand for support in a high-street branch, but it certainly isn't fine when a user is trying to find and navigate a service on their own.

The internet has changed the way that we access and use services, and our expectations around doing so, even if that service is not actually used online.

Regardless of how your service is consumed, the internet is where your users start, probably on their own and, based on global internet usage patterns, probably on a mobile device. Google (or their equivalent search engine) will be where they start, and then on to homepage to your service. The major challenge this creates is that your user will start by looking for what they think they need, not what you've decided they need.

If what they find is something that doesn't match this, or requires prior knowledge to be able to use, they will go elsewhere (if they can) or seek another way of getting support to use your service – probably over the phone. Either way, your revenue is likely to go down, or the cost of your service will go up. Pre-internet era services still account for the vast majority of the services we use, and were designed for a very different world to the one we now live in. But changing our services to be 'of the internet' rather than 'on the internet' has happened at a slower rate than the internet itself has changed. This is partially because we often don't rely on a new technology until that technology is ubiquitous. Since we don't have one clear definition of this, the more cautious organisations often lag well behind, waiting until the majority of their customers use a particular technology before changing their services. This means that services often keep a channel as a back-up long after the technology has ceased to be the main means of access for users, which in turn leads us to try to run the same service in multiple channels, without thinking of how that service would work natively in its new environment.

The simple fact that our services weren't designed for the channel they're delivered in is one of the most common causes of service failure.

A timeline of services

1800s: letters
Services first started to be accessible remotely through direct correspondence to the service provider.

1920s: forms
These letters of request started to become codified into 'forms' to improve the speed and accuracy of people responding to requests.

1960s: forms + support
With the first call centres becoming popular means of supporting customers, remote support started to be added to larger services, such as insurance and banking.

1970s: process + forms + support
With the introduction of computerised processes, the 1970s heralded a new way of seeing a service. No longer a set of instructions given to staff, computers started to make some decisions about our services for us. Making sure that records were accessible to staff meant having account numbers and an increasing number of unique IDs to identify users.

1980s: process + forms + customer service
The 1980s saw a rapid expansion of consultancies and methodologies to deal with the numbers of services now operating with remote support. The term 'customer experience' was first used to describe the growing need to make sense of the complexity of modern services. These were still mostly manual input, and the 'form' still dominated as the main means of interaction.

How services work now

Services today are composed of small component pieces joined together through data or user experience to form a seamless user journey that helps a user achieve their goal.

The goal that a service helps you to achieve can be very large – like buying a house – or it can be very small – like getting lunch. Either way, it will be broken down into smaller parts that help you achieve that overall goal.

Services in the internet age are not only defined by the user who's looking for them, but composed of 'small pieces loosely joined' as David Weinberger predicted in 2002. For example, when you're embarking on the goal of buying a house you might find that you need to complete several very distinct steps in order to be able to achieve it – like hiring a surveyor. Those steps themselves will then be broken down into smaller tasks. For example, when getting a survey done, you might need to first book a time for that survey to be done, then pay for it and review the final result.

In that way, each service is broken down into steps, and each step into a series of tasks. Each one of these steps or tasks will probably be called 'a service' by the person running it. What defines the edge of a service is very dependent on your context, so if all you do all day everyday is provide surveys, it's easy to think of the service as providing surveys.

While it's important for each step and task to be well-designed, it doesn't mean that these things are services. The only person who gets to decide what the service is, is the person who has the goal they need to achieve – and that's your user. It's your job to orchestrate all of the pieces of this service in as seamless a journey as possible, even if you don't provide the whole service yourself.

Designing services that are defined by user needs can seem like a daunting prospect. These services could be very large, and involve multiple different organisations to string together. It's important therefore to have some sense of how to break down a service into its component parts so that each 'loosely joined' piece can be designed in the context of the whole service.

Your user defines what your 'service' is

Designing how each of these pieces works together to help a user to achieve an end goal is not only possible, but vital to the success of a service.

Service: for example, buy house
A service is something that helps someone to do something. Only your user can determine what the service is.

Steps: for example, get a survey
Step are the things your user needs to do in order to achieve their overall goal. Crucially, steps should be introduced to a service where your user needs visibility and control over what happens next. For example, it would be incredibly unnerving to be able to do all of the things needed to buy a house in one seamless step.

The separate steps within the service of selling your house and buying a new one give you visibility and control over important decision points – like deciding which house to buy, how much money you want to spend or how many bedrooms you might need for any children. All of these steps are separate within the overall service of buying a house for the good reason that time and consideration are needed to make these decisions. This is why different organisations often fulfil different steps within the service. The break between those different organisations (if it works well) act as a natural point for consideration of information and decision-making.

Tasks: for example, check your survey
Tasks are the individual things you need to do to complete a step. How many steps or separate interactions your service has will depend on how many decision points your user has to make to achieve the desired outcome.

What makes a good servi

s

d

ce?

When Jordan Haignes started to get phone calls from Citigroup about repaying a loan, he didn't know why. He was annoyed. The bank, it seemed, thought he owed them $15,000. But Jordan hadn't ever taken out a loan with Citigroup. After some investigation, it transpired that, like millions around the globe before him, he had been the victim of identity fraud. Someone had taken his name, address, date of birth and other information and run up a bill of thousands on a credit card in his name. He complained, why had Citigroup agreed to give this fake Jordan a credit card, and why, now that the fraud was discovered, was it his job to sort it out?

The answer lies in our fundamentally different views on what we expect from services, in contrast with our expectations of almost anything else in our lives.

Any person in the US who is a victim of identity fraud is legally required to prove that their identity has been stolen in order to not be held liable for any damage done by that impersonator – and yet service providers don't suffer these penalties when they fail to identify users correctly.

This is a problem that stretches across the banking services sector and beyond, and it shows that, not only are the providers of services often not culpable for the failure of their service, they're often unwittingly involved in engineering its failure themselves – whether they know it or not.

Katy Highland was one such victim of accidental service sabotage. A teacher from New Rochelle, New York, Katy took out a loan when she went to college to pay for her teaching degree. When she graduated, she soon found herself struggling to repay her loan with two small children on a teacher's tiny salary.

She called her loan company, Naviant – one of the many organisations the US government outsources loan management to – and was offered to pause the payments on her loan.

Thinking this was her only option, she paused her payments.

What Katy didn't realise was that there was a government scheme that meant that – as a teacher – she was eligible to write off the remainder of her loan if she paid 120 consecutive payments on time. Every time she deferred her payments to Naviant, she was racking up interest and disqualifying herself from the scheme. So why, when this clearly wasn't the best thing for her to do, was she repeatedly told to defer her payments every time she called Naviant?

As it turns out, Naviant, like many organisations, has a strict limit on the amount of time a call centre operator can spend on the phone with a customer without losing their bonus. In this case, it's 7 minutes.

What with the numerous identity checks, surveys and statutory notices that need to be made to meet company policy, that 7 minutes becomes more like 5 – not much time to give high-quality advice to someone like Katy. In fact, almost the only thing you can do in 5 minutes on the phone to Navient – apart from complain – is to defer your loan. So this is what happened to Katy.

From top to bottom, everyone involved in providing this service to Katy, and the millions like her, is incentivised to provide a service that harms both individual users and society as a whole. Naviant was being incentivised by the US government to provide a cheap service, not an effective one, just as each call centre operator was incentivised to get Katy off the phone as quickly as possible. No one was focused on making sure that Katy could afford to keep teaching.

Individually, these can all seem like accidents, 'just the way the service works'. But at some point, they were all conscious decisions that add up to a service that neither meets the needs of individual users nor the goals of the organisation providing it. Someone decided to implement a 7-minute rule on the call centre and keep it there, despite the length of time each person needs to spend on customer identity checks. Someone decided not to train all staff in the government scheme that would have meant that Katy could have written off her loan.

As of 2018, 44 million Americans owed a total of $1.5 trillion in student loans. About 4 million of those Americans are already in default and a large number are on their way. At the same time, the US is facing an unprecedented shortage of teachers – caused, in part because of the low wages and high expectations of formal education.

These things happen because we don't design services, we let them happen by accident. The services we use everyday, from student loans to healthcare and housing, are more likely to be the product of technological constraints, political whim

Good services are designed

and personal taste than they are the conscious decision of an individual or organisation. By not designing our services, we're accepting that they will simply evolve to the conditions around them, regardless of whether or not that means a service meets user needs, is financially sustainable or achieves a certain outcome.

In 1971, Victor Papanek wrote: 'There are professions more harmful than industrial design, but only a few'. At the time, he was right. Industrial design was and still is responsible for the mountains of fridges filling our landfill sites, our addiction to motor transport and fossil fuels and our love of disposable food packaging. But perhaps even Papanek couldn't have foreseen the damage that could be done by bad services today.

The problems that bad services cause are vast – and they don't just have a negative impact on users, but cause problems to businesses and society as a whole. Unlike the problems with the products we use though, problems with services are often hard for us to identify and even harder to attribute.

In the UK government, about 80% of the cost of government is spent on services. Not surprising, given it is the oldest and largest service provider in the UK. Of the 10,000 recorded services (not all are known), some are over 200 years old, with the oldest recorded dating back to Henry VIII. What is more surprising perhaps is that up to 60% of the cost of these services is spent on service failure – phone calls asking government how to do something, or pieces of casework where forms aren't filled in correctly.

Spending on public services amounts to roughly a third of UK GDP, meaning that bad service design is one of the biggest unnecessary costs to UK taxpayers. And yet, it's not simply users that are paying the price for bad service design, it's our organisations too. We are footing the bill for the unnecessary phone calls, the returned products, complaints or missed appointments as much as our users.

A better service for users is generally a better service for an organisation to supply. So how is it that services continue to work in this way? It isn't because we don't want services to be better, or that we aren't aware that they need to work for users (you're reading this book, after all!). The answer is that services, unlike almost anything else that has an equivalent effect on our lives, have remained unrefereed and unscrutinised.

We have a collective blindness for services. They are the gaps between things, and so not only do we fail to see them, but we fail to recognise when they aren't working. They are often provided by multiple organisations, or parts of an organisation, so their cost and the negative effect they have on the world is more difficult to track than the cost of failing technology.

Service failure is hidden in wrongly worded questions, broken links and poorly trained staff; in emails not sent, phone lines that have been closed or inaccessible PDFs. In short, it's hidden in the small, everyday failures of our services to meet the very basic needs our users have – to be able to do the thing they set out to do.

Many of the problems with our services are not as obvious to spot as the problems with student loans or credit card sign-up in the US – but they are no less impactful in our users' lives. Each time we decide to incentivise our staff, change a policy, open or close a channel or buy a new piece of internal technology, we make a decision that will have an impact on the quality of the service for a user. We need to turn these everyday decisions into conscious design decisions, with the full awareness of the effect they will have on the service we provide, but we can only do that if we know what we want to achieve – what a good service is and what it isn't.

Each of the 15 principles in this book reflects one aspect of how to achieve 'good' for your users, your organisation and the world as a whole, but above all, it's crucial to remember that making something good for users, as we should all strive to do, is completely dependent on making something good for your organisation and for the world as a whole.

It's almost impossible to build a service that is good for the user if it's not good for your organisation and, likewise, if that thing isn't sustainable or doesn't have a positive impact on the world, it's not likely to be able to deliver long-term value for you or your users.

The principles in this book will give you a starting point in joining these three areas so that they work together. They aren't a complete list, and you will find your own, but I hope but they are a place to start.

Good services are:

Good for the user of the service
It does what they need it to do, in a way that works for them

Good for the organisation providing it
It's profitable and easy to run

Good for society as a whole
It does not destroy the world we live in, or negatively affect the society as a whole

15 prin
of goo
service

iples

design

No new ideas until everything's fixed

This is book is called 'good services' for a reason. It's not about 'great services', 'unique services', 'thrilling' or 'magical' services.

It won't tell you how to 'wow' your users with something they didn't expect, or build something that the world has never seen before – that's the job of user research, which you'll need to do to find out what they need from your unique service.

What this book will tell you is how to build something that meets the needs of your users, which they can find, understand and use without having to ask for help. It will tell you how to not disappoint your users, and make sure they can do the thing they set out to do. In a nutshell, it will help you to make services that work.

Building a service that works is a sorely undervalued activity of service design. In the rush to create something innovative, both old and new services often forget a user's most basic needs. Confirmation emails aren't sent, explanations aren't clear and appointments aren't flexible. All of these things lead to a collective friction in our daily lives that far outweighs any 'magical' or 'delightful' moments we might get from a small handful of services.

So what exactly makes a service 'good'? Ask most people this question and you will very often get the response of 'it depends'. But this assumption that all services are completely unique and that there are no similarities between them is wrong.

There are things that we all need from nearly every service we interact with, regardless of what it helps us to do. Things like being able to find that service and use it unaided, regardless of your knowledge or abilities. Or being able to do the thing you set out to do, without having to navigate the bureaucracies created by multiple organisations, or the strange effects of bad staff incentivisation. From luxury hotel check-ins to cancer treatment, from dog grooming to house selling, we need services that work. Services that are findable, usable and benefit our lives and the lives of everyone else around us.

Unlike many other forms of design, though, what makes a good service isn't a matter of personal taste. A service either works or it doesn't.

Ask a graphic designer to tell you what makes 'good' graphic design and you will get a different answer each time, but at least they'll give you an answer. That answer will crucially be based on well-known industry-held ideas of best practice that are taught in design schools across the world – things like the grid system, basic principles of typography or use of iconography. Yet despite the fact that what makes a good service isn't as subjective, service design has traditionally had no such understanding of best practice.

Almost 80% of the UK's economy is generated from services, a figure closely mirrored by the rest of Europe and North America. The industry of service design (depending on who you ask) is between 15–20 years old and yet, instead of defining what we mean by a good service, we've focused on how to design them.

This has led to the creation of a seemingly endless list of books and courses filled with methodologies and diagrams, and no answer to the most basic question: 'what is a good service?'

Because of this, we spend vast quantities of our time fighting for the legitimacy of service design. After all, how many other professions or activities are unable to answer the question: 'what does doing your job well look like?'

We need to move beyond this. Not so that we can replace user research or design with standards, but so that we can focus our efforts on learning and responding to the things that are unique about our services, not relearning the things that aren't.

This book isn't a to-do list of everything that will make your service work for you and your users – here will be things you will find along the way that are unique to your organisation or service – but it will tell you where to start.

The principles in this book have been crafted from years of experience working on some of the best and worst services in the world and honed by thousands of contributors around the globe who want to answer the question – what does it mean to make a service that works for users?

~~It depends~~

There are some things we all need from all services

1

A good service is easy to find

The service must be able to be found by a user with no prior knowledge of the task they set out to do. For example, someone who wants to 'learn to drive' must be able to find their way to 'get a driving licence' as part of that service unaided.

The first step in providing a good service is making sure that your user can find your service. This might sound simple, but it's a lot harder to do than it sounds.

Staff at a small rural UK county council discovered this to their horror in late 2016 when, after opening their information desk at 9am on a Tuesday, they were approached by a man carrying a dead badger. The man slammed the badger down on the desk, much to the shock of the customer services manager, proclaiming that he had found it outside of his house, and didn't know what to do with it. 'I tried looking on the website,' he said. 'But I couldn't find "dead badger" on the list, so I came here.'

Not every situation is as hard to figure out as what you need to do when disposing of a dead animal. After all, it's not something that happens every day. However, just as the man with the badger did, your users will come to your service with a preformed goal that they want to achieve. This can be very simple, like 'dispose of a dead animal' or 'learn to drive' or 'buy a house'.

Where your user starts will depend on how much they're already aware of what services might be available to meet their needs. Your job is to make sure that they can get from this goal to the service you provide, without having to resort to support. Or dropping off a dead badger at reception.

To a user, a service is simple. It's something that helps them to do something – like learn to drive, buy a house or become a childminder. This means that, to a user, a service is very often an activity that needs to be done. A verb that comes naturally from a given situation, which will more than likely cut across websites, call centre menus and around carefully placed advice towards its end goal. The problem is, this isn't how most organisations see their services. For most organisations, services are individual discrete actions that need to be completed in a specified order – things like 'account registration', 'booking an appointment' or 'filling a claim'.

Because these isolated activities need to be identifiable for the people operating them, we've given them names, nouns, to help us keep track of them and refer to them internally. Over time these names become exposed to users, even if we don't mean them to be initially.

In government, these are things like 'Reporting of Injuries, Diseases and Dangerous Occurrences Regulations 1995

Good services are verbs

Bad services are nouns

Google is the homepage of your service

(RIDDOR)' or 'Statutory Off Road Vehicle Notification (SORN)' – but the names private organisations give these things are no less obtuse. Names like 'eportal' or 'claims reimbursement certificate' are commonplace in the private sector.

Without understanding what our users are trying to achieve, and reinterpreting our services in language that our users can understand, we often place users in a situation where, to find something, they need to know exactly what they're looking for. For a user to find a service like RIDDOR or SORN, they first need to know what you call your service, resulting in an additional step being added to your service – that of learning the name that your organisation calls the thing they're trying to do.

As with the case of the dead badger, the less you know about the situation you're in, the support available to you or what you should do, the harder you will find this search. Needless to say, even the most patient people wilt at the prospect of this almost impossible task. Instead their confusion drives to them to call centres or, worse, they won't use your service at all.

Google is the homepage for your service. Whether your service is usable online or not, this is likely to still be the way that it will be found and accessed. When it comes to finding your service, nothing is more important than its name. Beyond making it easier for search engines to index and list your service, the name of your service makes a statement to your user about what that service does for them.

The UK Ministry of Justice found this out when they set about changing its Fee Remissions service in 2017. The Fee Remissions service helps to pay for or subsidise the cost of court fees for people who aren't able to pay themselves. However, it doesn't take a genius to realise that the word 'remission' is not the most frequently used word, particularly in a financial content. Given that the financial literacy of those applying often wasn't high, the title of the service was not only hard to understand for most people, but served to weed out precisely the users who were eligible to use it.

The reason this happened is simple, and happens every day in the creation of services. The title of the policy, somewhere long ago, had simply been made into the name of the service, without a thought to what language a user might use.

Nouns are for experts

Verbs are for everyone

Several rounds of research with the users of the service and staff providing it revealed that it was often referred to as 'help with court fees' rather than 'fee remissions', so the team renamed the service, meaning that users with low levels of financial literacy were able to use it.

When we design services with noun-based names like 'Fee Remission', we are designing them for use by experts, something that worked well when services were provided by trained expert humans, but means that they don't work unassisted on the internet.

Instead we often find that other professionals willingly offer support to our users – at a cost. This happened with Fee Remissions, as it so often does with many of the more obtuse services, from insurance buying to visa applications – when several third-party providers offered their services in helping users apply for what should have been a free service.

In the past, we used advertising to 'educate users' in our nouns, forcing the kind of brand familiarity that came naturally to well-used objects like Sellotape, Hoovers or Biros. But unless you're confident that you will get the kind of market ubiquity that comes from being a household name (and this happens to fewer companies than you'd think), your service is likely to be one of the thousands a user will use infrequently or once in their lives.

Equally, if you're a household name that has more than one service, this tactic is out. Your users still need to be able to sift through the many things you do to find the one thing that they need, and they aren't going to be able to do that if you've got a jumble sale of nouns to wade through.

Naming your service

Rather than using the words your organisation uses to describe the tasks it has completed, try to find out some of the words your user would use to describe what they're trying to achieve. What names work for users will depend on two things:

1   What your user wants to achieve

2   How knowledgeable they are about what services might be available to help them achieve their end goal

For example, someone moving house might not think that the service 'move house' exists, based on their previous experiences, but instead might think to look for 'removal companies' or 'estate agents'.

In areas where a service is less ubiquitous than moving house – for example, registering a trademark – a user's knowledge of what they might be able to get help with might be so low that they may try to find the noun they think most applies to them and hope for the best. This obviously means they may end up using service that isn't applicable to them. Your job is to understand how that overall task breaks down into smaller tasks a user identifies as something they need help with.

It might help to think about the name of your service existing somewhere on a spectrum between verb and noun, where the thing users think to look for will inevitably be somewhere in the middle. Most importantly, base your name on a solid understanding of the words your users use.

1   Avoid legal or technical language
    For example, rather than 'fee remission' use 'help with payment'.

2   Describe a task, not a technology
    Avoid words that describe a technology or an approach to technology that your service uses, such as 'portal', 'hub' 'e-something' or 'i-something'. Your approach to technology is rarely of interest to your user, and words

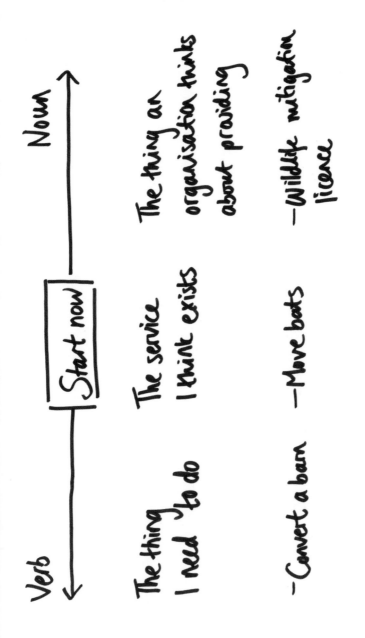

Verb ← → Noun

[Start now]

The thing I need to do

The service I think exists

The thing an organisation thinks about providing

—Convert a barn

—Move bats

—Wildlife mitigation licence

When searching for a service, what users look for is somewhere on a spectrum between what your organisation calls your service and what your user needs to do.

Changing what you call your service will change what it does

like these only serves to date your service to a particular
era of technology.

3   Don't use acronyms
    Acronyms might make it easier for you to refer to your
    service, but they are the most impenetrable language
    for your user to decipher.

Most importantly, changing the name of your service might
sound like a small thing, but aside from the huge effect on your
immediate users, it will have a big effect on what your service
does and how it operates in the long term.
     Seeing your service as 'stop paying tax on a vehicle' instead
of 'SORN' subtly shifts the purpose of that service closer to
what a user understands as its purpose and the language your
organisation uses to talk about it.

In summary

1   When it comes to finding your service, nothing is
    more important than its name
2   The name should reflect what users are trying to do
3   Use words that your users will understand

2

A good service clearly explains its purpose

The purpose of the service must be clear to users at the start of using the service. That means a user with no prior knowledge must understand what the service will do for them and how it will work.

One of the easiest mistakes people make when they're telling a story is to forget the beginning.

We've all been there; we're sat in a bar with a friend, or watching a colleague give a presentation, and we realise halfway through the story they're telling that we have no idea what it is they're talking about. They've missed out where they were, who they were with or a vital fact that the whole story hinges on.

It's an easy mistake to make, often because the audience we're talking to is familiar, and we presume a piece of prior knowledge from them that they don't have. The more familiar the audience, the more likely we are to forget.

The same goes for services. Sometimes we think our service is so familiar or ubiquitous that we forget to explain the most essential part of our service – what the service does.

The UK Driver and Vehicle Licencing Agency (DVLA) has experienced this problem with its 'report a medical condition' service. It's hugely important that people who are driving on the roads around us are fit to do so, but we will all experience some form of medical issue at some point in our lives that may affect our ability to operate a vehicle. When this happens, the DVLA monitors your situation and allows you to return to driving if and when you're fit to do so.

Most reports are made by people who report a medical condition that does need to be reported – things that affect your driving like having epilepsy or a stroke. However there's a minority – and quite a sizable minority (close to 40% in fact) – who report medical issues that, if treated, don't need to be reported at all. Things like ingrown toenails, broken bones and even miscarriages are reported by users who'd rather be safe than sorry when it comes to being on the right side of the law and their insurer.

The problem wasn't just that users didn't know which medical conditions to report, the problem was bigger than that. They didn't understand why they were reporting those conditions in the first place. If they had known that they were supposed to be reporting issues that affected their vision, attention or motor skills to check if they could still drive safely, then it's highly unlikely so many ingrown toenails would have been reported!

Not knowing the purpose of the service led users who didn't need to use the service to use it anyway, meaning that thousands of declarations in the system led to delays in reviewing the cases of users who did need to have their condition monitored.

Realising this, the service design teams at DVLA set about identifying the conditions that were the most misreported and created a medical reporting tool that would allow users to be clearly rejected from the system if they reported something like a skin condition or toenail issue. More importantly than this, they explained at the beginning of the service why they were asking for this information, and what the purpose of the service was.

By being clear about the purpose of the service, DVLA ensured that those who needed to use it received the attention they needed, rather than falling to the bottom of the pile, and that those who didn't need to use it didn't waste their time.

But this rule of making clear the purpose of your service, and therefore who should use it, doesn't just apply to a public service context. It's easy to see how, if a service isn't applicable to a user who would like to use it (for example, it can't be delivered in their area) that it could become frustrating. As how your service works is such a large part of your user's experience, it's often vitally important to make it clear to your user *exactly* how it works.

Ofo, a global bicycle-sharing scheme, discovered this when, after introducing its bikes to London, it found that a large number of bikes were seemingly available to users, but nowhere to be seen. After further investigation, the problem revealed itself: users were storing bikes in their gardens, porches and on balconies to ensure they always had access to it when they needed it.

There was nothing in the description of Ofo's service to explain how the scheme worked, or what it was for, that would explain to users why you shouldn't hoard a bike on your balcony.

Purpose of your service =
what your service does
why it does it
how it does it
who it's for

When you're making the purpose of your service clear, you'll need to think about four distinct things – what your service does, why it does that thing, how it works and who it's for.

These things form a picture of what the purpose of your service is. For example, your service may be 'dry cleaning' like any other, but when that dry cleaning is collected from your user's doorstep and returned in an hour, that service has a very different purpose and therefore value to your user than the average high-street dry cleaners. When thinking about how you'll explain this to your users, it's important not to forget about these four elements, and not to make one more prominent than the other. In the DVLA example we can see that it explained what the service did and how it worked, but barely touched who the service was for, let alone why the service did what it did in the first place.

Explaining how your service works without clearly explaining what it does and your service will come across as either disingenuous or confusing. Like an advert for a new type of tool on a shopping channel that sounds brilliant, but isn't clear what it actually does.

Likewise, if you don't explain 'how' your service works, your users can presume complexity and difficulty at worst, or inconvenience at best, basing the expectation of your service on their experience of your competitors. Taking our dry cleaners as an example of this, you might expect your new door-to door dry cleaners to need dropping off and picking up, unless you know that this isn't how the service works.

Services are increasingly competing on 'how' they provide their service, not what their service does. Uber, Deliveroo and Airbnb are all perfect examples of this, taking the traditional services of taxis, food delivery and short-term accommodation booking and delivering them in a convenient way that increases their value to users. However, unless they describe why they do what they do, who their service is for and what their service does, these efforts fall just as flat as DVLA trying to get the right users to register a medical condition.

When considering these things, ask yourself the following four questions and make sure they are clear to users at all points of the journey:

What does the service do?

Clearly express what the service tangibly does for your user. Be factual, avoid marketing promises. Stick to the functionality. What outcome will it achieve for the user?

How does the service work?

Sometimes how your service works is almost as important as what it does. Who is able to use it? How is it paid for? Is it a subscription or a one-off purchase? How quickly can you do the thing you're offering? What is it about the way your service works that makes it quicker or more convenient for your users than any other? Are there any other benefits to your service besides basic convenience? Is your service sustainable or funded/made in a way that benefits society at large?

Who is the service for?

This will probably be obvious to your user if you express what the service does and how it does it well enough, and explain that it's not possible to users who aren't eligible or suitable for the service to be moved out of the journey as soon as possible.

A service's form follows a service's function

Why does the service exist?

Possibly the most crucial of all: make sure you explain to your users why your service exists and what outcome it will achieve, both personally for the user and for society. This is particularly relevant for public services where a user is being asked to do something that they otherwise wouldn't consider doing. For example, it's a lot easier to understand why you need to report a medical issue to the DVLA if you know that you have to declare conditions that make you a danger to other drivers.

When trying to make the purpose of your service clear to your users, it's easy to automatically leap to written explanations – long 'read me' instructions that explain the process or, at the very least, a 'how to' that explains the basics.

Yet the statement that Chicago architect Louis Sullivan coined in 1896 is no less true of services than it was of buildings – 'form follows function'. If we design services in a way that shows their function, it's easier for users to understand the purpose of a service at first glance in the way that they might understand the purpose of a building from the way it looks. This is a principle that product design has taken to heart and meant that, to a greater extent than ever before, products with a clear purpose have avoided the need for marketing in the same way as their competitors have in the past.

You only need to look at Apple iPhone adverts to understand that what they're showing users is a very clear purpose and functionality, not a vacuous sales pitch about how great their thing is compared to the competition.

Users are increasingly looking to services to be clear about their purpose as a means of reassurance of whether they should use it. But just as this is clear by looking at any good product, so it should be for services.

When thinking about how to make sure the purpose of your service is clear, you have three things at your disposal:

1   The name of your service
    As we covered in principle 1, making sure that your service is findable by clearly describing what the service is for in its name is important. Sometimes this name will be a sub-service of a larger service. For example, Airbnb may

have sub-services named 'make a booking' or 'list your house' that clearly describe what they do for users.

2   The description of your service

Often when designing your service you will have the opportunity to describe it. Use this opportunity sparingly as your user often doesn't have a lot of time to spare at this stage of using a service. Good products don't need instruction manuals, and neither do services, so try not to see this as instructions for your service. Stick to the information that describes the value your service brings to your user.

3   Other heuristic elements of your service

How your service works can be encoded in the way that your user interacts with it. For example, a large 'subscribe' button on your homepage is a clear indication that your service is paid for by subscription. Think about the way that your service looks and acts, and what messages this gives your user about who it's for, what it does or how it works.

In summary

1   Think about what your service does for users, why it does this, how it does it and who it does this for.
2   Clearly communicate this to users – through things like the service name, description and even the interface of how it works.

The product is the service is the marketing

Russell Davies, former GDS head of marketing

3

A good service sets the expectations a user has of it

A good service must clearly explain what is needed from the user to complete the service and what that user can expect from the service provider in return. This includes things like how long something will take to complete, how much it will cost or if there are restrictions on the types of people who can use the service.

In 2017, the City of San Jose launched a new digital service for residents to report potholes, streetlight outages and graffiti. Like other '311 services' in North American cities, the goal was to make it easy for residents to report problems in their neighbourhood to government.

The service had been running for a year, when the team noticed some interesting data coming back from their call centre staff. Rather than decreasing the number of calls to the local city hall, the number of complaints about broken street lights and rusty park benches had strangely increased.

What could be the problem? Were neighbourhoods getting worse? In fact, something much simpler was going on. Through talking to users and city staff, the team realised that the increase in calls was not from people who were reporting an issue for the first time. Instead they were from people who had already reported something using the digital service, who were confused and frustrated by the fact that nothing had been done about it.

What the team had missed in their first iteration of the service was a way to let users know how long it might take to fix the issue they had reported. While this was fine for some things, like graffiti, which can be removed in days, this wasn't fine for something like a broken streetlight, which might take weeks for an engineer to fix, depending on the complexity of the fault. San Jose residents were frustrated because the digital service didn't let them know how long it would take to get something fixed. By not setting expectations for users, the team had set their service up to fail.

As we saw in principle 2, clearly explaining the purpose of your service is a vital part of helping your user to understand what to expect from a service, but the purpose of a service is by no means the only expectation a user might have when using your service.

How long something will take to complete, how much it will cost, whether they will be contacted and what else they might need to do after using your service are all things that a user needs to know to make a decision about whether or not to use your service.

Of the many management books published on the topic of 'service management', most will tell you that 'setting expectations' is the most important part of making sure your user is happy. What they argue is that if a user knows what's coming, they're more likely to be OK with their experience being awful. While this is probably true, it is neither a good bar to set for your service nor a good way of dealing with the variety of expectations your user might have.

Setting the expectations a user has of your service is no way to paper over the cracks of a badly designed service. Your service has an effect on your user's life. Whether that effect is big or small, knowing what to expect helps people to plan and take control of their situation. It gives them power – and in some cases the ability to make another choice if what you're offering isn't going to work for them.

If you don't tell them what to expect, then that small window of opportunity to take control – change their mind, take another route or make another choice – is gone and, with it, what power and agency they had over the situation.

The counterargument to this is of course that giving users a choice gives them more of an opportunity to go elsewhere, and to some extent it does, but this isn't a bad thing for you, even if your service is competitive.

Without clearly explaining what your service can and can't do, you risk people expecting something from your service that it can't deliver. These unhappy users will then need to contact you to understand why the thing they were expecting to happen hasn't. Users like this are expensive. Far better that they take one look at your service and don't use it if it's not suitable for them or it's not going to do what they need.

Understanding what expectations people have of your service

Before you get to work on how you're going to manage your users, expectations, it's important to understand what expectations they have in the first place. Most people base their expectations on past experiences, so if another company in another country has done something, the likelihood is someone is going to expect the same of you at some point.

If your service is transportation, for example, your user could expect you to pick up their luggage and drop it off for them, be able to get on and off your transport regularly without paying extra or defer their payment of the journey until later. Some of these might seem ludicrous to you, knowing what you do about your service, but they will seem perfectly reasonable to your user. There's no way that you can predict what expectations a user will have of your service without doing research, but you can predict the types of expectations your users will have of you and deal with these in the right way.

There are three types of expectation that you need to think about when you're designing your service:

Universal expectations

These are the things about your service that are fundamental to what you're delivering and are universal to almost all users because other similar services work in the same way. If you're a bank, almost all of your users expect to be able to withdraw money from an ATM any time they like, or pay for things using a card.

These are universal expectations that almost all users will have because all other banks work in this way. In fact, expectations like this are so universal that they become part of our collective cultural know-how, in the same way we know to walk on a pavement (if there is one) or wave our hand under a sensor-controlled tap. They become universal truths we all expect from similar services. They are often globally recognisable but, where they're not, they will be ubiquitous to a particular region.

Assumed expectations

These are the things that people don't know about your service and will therefore assume (rightly or wrongly). These are usually things that aren't universally known. Things like the fact that in the UK, there is a delay between signing up to a new electricity provider and getting your first bill (just in case you change your mind), or that you need two forms of ID to open a bank account.

When someone doesn't know what to expect, then an assumption usually takes its place. These are usually assumptions that are easier or more convenient for the user. The things that cause your users to have these assumed expectations tend to be the things that vary between you and your competitors (one sends out a bill immediately and another doesn't), or the things that you wouldn't know from watching films or chatting to your friends and family.

If your service is used infrequently by people (creating a will, for example) or by very few people (like registering a pedigree dog), you're much more likely to be susceptible to these types of expectations from new users.

Outlier expectations

These are the things that only some users might expect, based on a previous experience of a similar service elsewhere, and can very often be based on a better experience a user might have had.

Taking banking as an example, this might include users getting instant notifications on their phone when they spend using your card. Because of this, it's common for outlier expectations to evolve to become tomorrow's universal expectations as users with these new expectations use your service.

How to 'manage' expectations

These three types of expectation need to be dealt with differently.

You won't need to explain universal expectations to users when they sign up to your service. Doing this is a bit like advertising that your restaurant serves food, or your bathrooms have toilet paper. It might be true but proudly explaining that your service does the absolute basics will make your user doubt your ability to deliver those basics, let alone anything more advanced.

You will need to monitor these closely, though, because if any universal expectations aren't met at any point, they will have the most severe effect on your user. If this is the case, tell your users immediately so that they can make other arrangements.

So far, so straightforward. Assumed expectations are much more tricky. These are the things that are the most important to explain upfront to your users, because although they're obvious to you, they won't be to your users unless they're experts. Here you have two options – you can either design these expectations out (that is, change your service so that it's simpler or closer to what most users will expect) or explain clearly to your users what to expect.

Nothing is as effective as making sure that your service is as simple as possible to use and works in a way that is expected, but if this isn't possible, and sometimes it isn't, make sure that you identify your assumed expectations and explain as clearly as you can (at the point that expectation becomes important to your user) what they should expect.

Be very wary of explaining to the point you end up requiring your user to educate themselves in your process before they start. Doing this puts all the responsibility on the user, and means they'll either not bother to read your carefully written instructions (when was the last time you read a manual from cover to cover?) or give up on your service entirely.

Outlier expectations need to be dealt with completely differently to the other two. You won't need to consider them in your service now, but you do need to watch out in the future.

Almost overnight, the expectations of a few can become the expectations of many. A new paradigm enters the market and what seemed an unreasonable expectation becomes something that's expected by everyone and your service is in trouble.

British bank Monzo is a perfect example of this. As an app-first bank, it was able open accounts with a user's selfie and a passport scan, and provide instant notifications of transactions. It's taken years for the banking sector to catch up with this 'new' expectation that users have of instant visibility and access to their finances, and it's a battle many are still losing.

It's important to consider all three types of expectations when designing a service, and not to focus on just one to the detriment of the others.

It's common, for example, to obsess over meeting your user's universal expectations, to the extent that you don't notice the slew of outlier expectations creeping up behind you. Never dismiss your users' outlier expectations, as they may become your next universal expectation. Equally, focusing too much on outlier expectations, by wanting to make your service work in new and innovative ways, can also lead to missing important universal expectations. These are critical to meet as, without these, your user will see little value in your service.

Assumed expectations are also important to deal with. It's normal to feel dismayed and confused by your users' expectations if they don't match your current service, seeing them as 'unreasonable', 'unachievable' or even 'stupid'. But while you may not be able to meet those expectations, it's important to acknowledge them and openly deal with them.

So, to design a good service, always meet your user's universal expectations, try to reduce as many of their assumed expectations as possible and keep a firm eye on outlier expectations so that you're ahead of the curve when some of these become universal.

In summary

1   Understand what expectations users might have of your service.
2   Work out whether these are 'universal', 'assumed' or 'outlier' expectations.
3   Try to meet as many of these expectations as you can. If you can't, explain to the user why not.

4

A good service enables a user to complete the outcome they set out to do

A good service helps the user to achieve a goal – be that start a business, learn to drive or move house – in as much of a seamless stream of events as possible. This starts from the moment that a user is considering doing something to the moment they have achieved their goal, including any steps needed to support the user after they have reached their goal.

Now that we've understood what we need to do to make sure that our service works well for users before they use it, we can now turn our attention to the equally important task of making sure that these users can actually use your service. The most basic element of this by far, is making sure they can achieve what they set out to do. While this might seem like the simplest, and therefore easy, thing we can do to make sure our service works well, it's very often the hardest part of building a good service.

By understanding the way your users discover your service and set their expectations around it, you will have learned two important lessons:

1   That your user defines what a service is by what it is they want to achieve.
2   The way your user thinks and talks about your service is likely to be different to the way that you do.

Because of this, what your user expects from your service when they arrive at it is very often not the same as the service you provide. What a user looks for, as we saw in principles 1 and 3, is based on their knowledge and understanding of the task at hand, and on their expectations on what services might be available to help them achieve their goal.

Your service might support all of the tasks a user needs to do to achieve their goal, or it might provide only a tiny sliver of those things. What's important isn't the scope of what you provide, but whether or not the part of the journey you provide helps your user to reach their ultimate goal.

All too often, we become myopic about our services over time and forget that what we're trying to do is help someone to achieve something, rather than complete the small part of the end task we provide.

When someone's trying to buy a house, for example, they might need to employ a solicitor, but that doesn't mean that 'employ a solicitor' is their end goal.

Designing a service in these conditions is hard. But it is the reality of designing a service in the world we now live in, where the goals we have in life are provided by an increasingly complex combination of providers.

When we haven't considered all of the steps involved in helping our users to meet their end goal, or designed a service that integrates with those other parts of a service, users either fail to achieve their goal or frequently arrive at your service in the wrong order, needing help to start at the beginning.

For example, they might have put an offer in on a house without securing a mortgage or conducting a survey of the house they're intending to buy. Your job as a provider of part of this service is to help every user orientate themselves within that end-to-end journey. This might seem like extra work, particularly if you only provide one small part of a service, but it is vital work as it means that when a user arrives at your part of that journey, they're doing so with the full ability to be able to take part in using it, and continue their journey onwards to a satisfactory goal if they need to.

Your service will be more effective, better ranked, more efficient or more profitable if your user knows what they need to know by the time they get to you, and they're able to achieve what they set out to achieve.

When we fail to recognise and design for a user's true goal, our services can create negative consequences that are much more severe than just disorientating and confusing for our users. The worldwide issue of homelessness is a perfect example of this.

In 2006, *The New Yorker* published an article by Malcolm Gladwell that changed our understanding of the problem forever. In the article 'Million-Dollar Murray', Gladwell chronicled the life of a man living on the streets of Reno in Nevada, US. Gladwell calculated that the cost of Murray's time spent in prison, his stays in homeless shelters, his visits to emergency rooms and his stays in hospital added up to more than a million dollars in 10 years – the implication being that when people think we can get away with responding to homelessness 'on the cheap', it actually costs us more than the cost of solving the whole problem.

The article is important in that it highlights the real cost of our current response to homelessness, and has inspired communities and government officials to think differently. But what it also shows us is that when we try to solve one small part of a user's problem with one small slice of a service, we often don't achieve the results we set out to achieve. Often, the perceived cost saving we think we will achieve in providing a smaller part of a whole service is outweighed in the number of people who have to provide additional elements of their service to pick up the pieces. Our service might still be cheaper, but someone is picking up the bill elsewhere.

There are many different reasons someone might find themselves without a permanent home. Chronic or sudden illness, loss of a job, relationship breakdown or an abusive family situation can all mean that someone's housing situation can change rapidly and dramatically. These things can happen to any of us at any time, and with increasing house prices and decreasing levels of security and stability of housing, many more of us are finding ourselves without a permanent place to live. Whatever the cause of the situation, the goal of people in this circumstance is almost always universal – to find a safe and secure home.

What Gladwell discovered was that not only weren't we solving the whole problem for users, we weren't intervening early enough in their journey towards that need – precisely because we didn't understand this whole journey in the first place.

Finding a home takes coordination between multiple agencies, and a person can go through a huge number of interactions with the state before they find themselves on a list for rehousing. The average person who is homeless will see emergency care workers, drug and alcohol treatment centres and the police, all of whom aren't directly responsible for the end result of getting a person the housing they're looking for. In essence, not only is the service expensive overall because it is fragmented, but it starts too late and ends too soon, only providing the middle part that stops users from being in extreme crisis.

Gladwell is not the first or the last to point this out, but the message remains the same: when you're defining what your user wants to achieve, it's all too easy to only consider those things that fall strictly within the scope of the service you already provide.

As we can see with the case of homelessness in Nevada, doing this can mean that we create additional work for our users in navigating the silos between us and other providers. Or mean that we have to do extra work to find our way to a service in the first place – either way, the goal becomes much harder for our user to achieve and more costly for us to provide.

You can't change or alter your user's goal. But, even if the service you provide is one small part of a much larger journey, or in fact, designed to intercept that end-to-end journey (like a government regulation) it's important that what you provide works with all of the other elements of the end-to-end service a user might use to achieve their end goal. Doing this requires awareness and collaboration with people outside of your organisation – coordinating data, language and processes so that you are working well for a user.

As our lives become an ever-more-complex web of technology and services, integration of all of the parts needed to achieve a goal into one seamless service is increasingly important to users. We can see this in the increasing number of services whose sole job it is to make it easier to access other services as one seamless experience. British chatbot-based financial service Cleo does this for banking, by bringing your bank accounts together as one balance, and there are countless more like it in other sectors.

Making sure you're always focused on what your user is trying to achieve can not only mean that your service helps them to achieve their goal, but that you do too – as you stay focused on providing something that people need, not just the things you can do already.

A service is still a service even if you don't provide all of it

Thinking about whole services will change what your service is

Designing your service to fit within a wider user journey won't just help you to design a better service, it will help you to understand how your service might be delivered most effectively, discovering other elements of your service that aren't being provided by other organisations or, in extreme cases, change the way your service works fundamentally.

Urban navigation company Citymapper is a perfect example of this. As a company whose job it is to help you navigate around cities, it would have been very easy for Citymapper to look at the needs people have from each mode of transport on offer and work out a way to make it easier for users to use buses, trains and bicycles.

Instead, the company realised that what its users wanted wasn't to be able to use the bus more easily but to be able to get somewhere in either the least amount of time or with the least amount of effort. This meant that the service it provides is agnostic to the mode of transport on offer. Rather than offering users a complex list of transport options, Citymapper instead opted for a big button saying 'get me home'. It's Citymapper's job to help you navigate the complexity of options available to you to meet your ultimate aim – of getting home – and that's bigger than just helping you to find the nearest bus.

When designing your service, try to ask yourself: is this really where our user starts? And: is this really where they reach their goal?

In summary

There is not one perfect way to make sure that your service helps
your users to do what they set out to do, but start by:

1   Understanding what your user is trying to achieve.
2   Get a good understanding of who else delivers parts of
    this service and how they relate to your organisation.
3   Look at your organisation's ability to deliver all of this
    service – if this isn't feasible, define what a rational scope
    for your part of that end-to-end service will be.
4   Consider which part of the service it makes sense to deliver
    first. Just because you've decided to deliver an end-to-end
    service doesn't mean you need to deliver it all at once.
    Start small and build or improve in increments.
5   Look at how data gets shared between the organisations
    delivering this service – are there things you could share
    that would make it easier for your user? Or things that
    you need from organisations that would enable you to
    provide a better service?

Design whole services
from end to end:
from when the user starts
trying to achieve a goal
to when they finish

From front to back:
the user-facing service
and internal processes

In every channel:
digital, phone, post,
face-to-face and
physical elements

5

A good service works in a way that's familiar

People base their understanding of the world on previous experiences. If there's an established custom for your service that benefits a user, your service should conform to that custom. But be mindful that not all customs benefit users – some have been put in for the benefit of the organisation running the service, rather than users. Avoid customs that negatively affect your user or those that are inefficient or outdated.

British trains have come to be known throughout the world for a number of reasons. From their iconic branding, designed by Design Research Unit in the 1960s, to their unreliability and perpetual lateness due to 'the wrong kind of snow' or 'leaves on the line'. Whether you feel positively or negatively about British trains, they have a notoriety that is almost unique.

In the UK, however, another more nefarious characteristic of our trains has become equally well-known – their toilets. Or, more specifically, the locks on the doors of the toilets. The notorious 'electric locking' doors used by many trains on the British rail network were first introduced in the early 2000s and were initially so complex to use that users would regularly be caught out by a fellow passenger opening the door while they were on the toilet, having not locked the door properly. Rather than a simple mechanism that provided users with visual feedback that the door was locked, the new, 'smart' toilet doors used a single button to close and lock the door. The only feedback that the door was locked was a flashing red or green lock symbol.

The complexity of these locks eventually became so farcical that Scottish soft drinks company Irn-Bru used the toilets on a British train as the scene for one of its most famous TV adverts – where a man fails to lock the door and, after falling out of the toilet with his trousers around his ankles, is handed a consolatory can of Irn-Bru by a refreshment trolley operator.

Realising this was a problem, train operators eventually produced signs to go alongside the doors, instructing users in how to operate them. These the signs soon led to YouTube instruction videos and audio announcements in the toilets – none of which, of course, solved the problem.

The problem wasn't that the train companies had failed to explain how the locks worked (after all, no other public bathroom has to do this) or that they tried something new. The problem was that the doors had taken a complete departure from the way that any other toilet door looked or worked. This meant users were stranded, with no previous experience to help them, and no reference for what to do next.

This kind of situation happens often in areas of design where there is very little change, and established ways of doing something almost by second nature.

Locks are one such example of this because there are very few new door locks being invented. This might be because the way we lock doors now is the pinnacle of perfection, honed over many hundreds of years of trial and error. But, more likely, it's because once something becomes a design pattern, it's very difficult to change it. Any change, no matter how much of an improvement, has to gain a certain amount of ubiquity to be able to be learned. In a nutshell, if every other door on every train around the world worked in the same way as the electric ones on British trains, we might have seen fewer red-faced train toilet users in the UK.

Services, in this instance, are no different to products. There are some elements in our services that are so universal that they are hard to change. Getting an email confirmation after buying something online, paying for a hotel room when you leave, or giving your phone number when you book a table at a restaurant are things we are so familiar with that they are hard to do differently.

But these 'patterns' to the way services work can happen at a much higher level, where services that are similar to one another work in the same way. Take buying a home or signing up to an online subscription for a newspaper – the experience is generally the same, whichever company you use.

We have set expectations when we enter into these interactions that are borne of years of experience of watching others complete the same tasks. These learned behaviours are often so strong that we will go along with a bad way of doing something, purely because we presume that 'this is just the way that it is'.

Occasionally, though, something might break out of these accepted ways of working and work in a completely different way. This can happen for a number of different reasons – your organisation can create a better way of doing something that becomes so ubiquitous that it defines how everyone else works – like Apple did with modern mobile phones or 4chan and Reddit have for internet chat rooms.

Or your service can discover a better way of doing something that, through openness and sharing, can be adopted by other service providers.

This is common practice with interaction design, where design patterns are created then deliberately reused by other designers.

But the same can be said of services (as we saw in principle 3) with the creation of 'outlier expectations' – things that some users might expect, based on a previous experience of a similar service elsewhere that works in a completely different way.

As discussed in that principle, British bank Monzo is a great example of this. Monzo was founded in 2015 (as Mondo), when the world of banking was still hugely manual and time-intensive – if you wanted to sign up for an account, you had to visit a branch, and if you wanted to make any significant changes, you'd need to speak to someone on the phone or in person.

Security measures were often laborious, with very little visibility or control over spending. Monzo decided to change this by introducing an app-based banking service that allowed you to sign up for an account instantly with just a selfie and a picture of your passport and, crucially, provided users with direct, instant feedback when transactions were made.

Although initially only prepaid debit cards were offered, Monzo was so successful that it soon started to offer current accounts. But Monzo wasn't successful just because it did something new but because this new thing was easier than what came before – unlike the doors on British train toilets. This is what we often call 'disruption', but these companies do more than simply disrupt markets, they set user expectations. What Monzo created was an outlier expectation that became universal.

We now live in a world in which, thanks to companies like Monzo, we expect banking transactions to be instantaneous and provide us with immediate feedback. We expect visibility of who we've paid, and the ability to make changes ourselves without the assistance of a member of staff. When something works in this way it can quickly scale from being 'niche but great' to being something that everyone expects, moving from just being used by early adopters to becoming mainstream. But outlier expectations can be set by bad experiences, too – in the case of the doors on British trains, most toilets on British trains now have comprehensive instructions on the locking mechanism, even if their door locks in a way that is perfectly easy to understand.

There is a delicate balance between working in a familiar way, and breaking out of this to set a better way of working. Try to do something new without properly testing it with users, and you risk creating a 'new' way of working that is unusable because users have no prior experience of it. Equally, sticking with a way of working that doesn't work for users just because that's what everyone else does can be just as damaging.

Sometimes we can so be reluctant to break out of this standardised way of working – even when the need to do so becomes overwhelming – that we can cause harm to our users.

This mistake very nearly cost us the world as we know it, when the US aerospace industry failed to come up with a solution to one of the biggest problems of the 1970s – skyjacking.

The 1970s were a golden age for skyjacking. Between 1968 and 1972, more than 130 aeroplanes were hijacked in the US alone. Some wanted to be taken to Cuba to join Fidel Castro's rising communist movement, others simply wanted money, but the problem became so commonplace that there was often more than one skyjacking a day.

Eventually, the problem became so bad that, to avoid more unscheduled flights to Cuba, the US Federal Aviation Administration (FAA) actually considered building a fake version of Havana airport in Florida. This boom in crime was facilitated by the fact that there was virtually no security at airports. What we now see as the completely normal process of walking through metal detectors and having your carry-on luggage searched simply wasn't a thing. Instead, airlines used a 'behavioural profile' to identify suspect passengers. Airline workers would give passengers the once-over before they flew, and if they met a list of more than 20 indicators of a potential hijacker, they would be subject to a private search. The characteristics were designed to single out just 1% of travellers, leaving the other 99% to carry on with their flight unchecked.

The FAA did everything in its power to avoid subjecting passengers to security checks. At the time, US airlines had a tremendous amount of political influence and, after a number of congressional hearings, airlines managed to use their political clout to stall reform.

The rationale was simple: this was the first really affordable era of mass air travel. If people felt like criminals merely because they wanted to travel on planes, or wait in line for 15, 20 or even 30 minutes, they might just choose to drive or take a Greyhound bus.

Instead the FAA tried to work around the problem from other angles, looking at solutions that ranged from inventive to downright weird. Alongside a fake Cuban airport, it solicited ideas from the public that included, among other things, making everyone wear boxing gloves on the plane so they couldn't hold a gun.

It took no less than the threat of nuclear devastation to change their minds. In November 1972, three men boarded Southern Airways Flight 49 and threatened to crash it into the nuclear research reactor at Oak Ridge National Laboratory in Tennessee. It was now clear that the risks of not implementing security at airports had far outstripped the need to conform to existing passenger expectations of what an airport experience should be, and on 5 January 1973, the FAA instituted universal physical screening of passengers.

On the first day, all the major newspapers sent their reporters to their local airports, hoping for confrontations. But, in reality, the public welcomed the change. Even though there were significant delays, and a complete change to their experience for air travel, there was such fear surrounding the criminal epidemic of hijackings that passengers welcomed the change. These changes were quickly adopted by other countries, who were experiencing smaller but similar issues.

Since then, the International Civil Aviation Organization has controlled airline security, making sure that whatever is implemented gets done universally. In short, making sure that what was an outlier expectation of security became a universal expectation of all passengers.

It's important to make changes that make your service better and safer for your users, even if this occasionally means a slightly different way of working. However, whatever change you make, it has to be understandable to users – in the case of security checks in the US, this was through an understanding of why this needed to be done and a lot of handholding. With Monzo, this was through good, simple design that was intuitive to use.

Crucially though, changes to expected ways of working in your service require a critical mass to be usable by all users. The bigger the shift from the norm, the more ubiquitous this will need to be for users to become familiar to be able to or want to use your changed service.

In the case of US air security, it wasn't simply US airlines that adopted the security checks. To do so would have created such a large security hole in the new system that it would've rendered it completely pointless. More importantly still, there would have been far more confusion and complaints from passengers if this system was only implemented in one country. Badly designed airports are a nightmare for passengers today, but imagine arriving in a new country that you have no idea how to get into or out of because 'airport security' simply isn't a thing in the country you came from.

It might seem obvious to us now that making a service consistent with our user's expectations (unless those expectations are damaging to the user or not as good as they could be) is a good thing. But it is rarely consistency with expectations we think of when we design a service.

More often than not, we don't think of our services in the context of the world around us and the other services a user has to interact with. If we do, we either think our users will get used to it eventually, or that we can change the way people understand the world, simply by the power of our service alone.

While it might be possible to change the expectations of users if you disrupt the market, and gain ubiquity in the process, this is beyond the reach of most established services. What is far more achievable is working iteratively towards something that both works well for your users, and is something that is recognisable. To do this means taking a look outside of your service and analysing what other equivalent services do, and reviewing whether their way of working is something you should adopt.

Importantly, if you decide to do something completely different, this will need to be both incredibly intuitive, and produced in such a way that it has a chance to be ubiquitous within your market. Doing this means being an active participant in a collective change, sharing your workings and talking about its benefits so that others can adopt that way of working.

As Cathy Casserly, former CEO at Creative Commons, said in 'The Future of Creative Commons' in 2013: 'today, not letting others use your work can mean irrelevance'. Or, in the words of the UK's Government Digital Service, 'make things open: it makes things better'.

Making sure your service works well, and in a way that is familiar to users, is a delicate balance.

So, in summary:

1   Research how your competitors work and look for patterns in what they do.
2   Understand if there is an easier, more intuitive or more effective way of doing what you're doing.
3   If there is, test it to understand how different this is from your users' existing expectations of how your service might work.
4   Make sure that any changes you make are intuitive.
5   Share the changes to the way your service works with others so that your pattern can become ubiquitous.

Make things open:
it makes
things better

UK Government Design Principles

6

A good service requires no prior knowledge to use

A service should not work in a way that assumes any prior knowledge from the user.

When Jennifer David travelled to New York to go to a conference, she decided to pack for every eventuality – some smart clothes for work, stuff to wear out on the town and more T-shirts than she needed for a month.

When she arrived at New York's JFK Airport, she picked up her bag and headed to the hotel. Deciding to unpack her clothes before heading out, she opened her suitcase, and it was then that Jennifer discovered, like millions of travellers before her, she had picked up the wrong piece of luggage.

Rather than her smart suits and dresses, she found a Celtic football strip, 4 pairs of boxer shorts, 5 pairs of white sports socks and...a single tab of Viagra. Whoever the bag belonged to was planning on an interesting weekend in the city.

Jennifer's immediate reaction was to speak the airline she'd travelled with and try to swap the bag she'd picked up by mistake with hers. It quickly became clear that recovering lost luggage wasn't a simple service to negotiate. The airline handed her to the airport, the airport passed her to airport authorities and, finally, to a little-known company called WorldTracer – which specialises in recovering lost luggage.

WorldTracer helps users to trace luggage that's been lost, regardless of the airline they travel with. Around 24.8 million pieces of luggage were 'mishandled' in 2018 and, with a complex web of airline companies, flight operators, airport authorities, local police, finding, identifying and returning lost luggage to users is big business.

Unless you worked in aviation you would have very little idea that a company like WorldTracer existed, but it is one example of a special type of service that exists entirely because of the failure of another kind of service.

Getting your luggage back without a service like WorldTracer would be long and complicated. It would mean negotiating lots of organisations you may not even know exist, in countries where you may not speak the language.

Services like WorldTracer exist because many of our services encourage expertise, even expect it of us. Like an old institutional building that is impossible to navigate, many of our services expect the people visiting them to have been there before and know their way around. They act like parasites would in nature, making a home in or around a failing service to provide something that users need. They join the dots, connect the pieces or negotiate the bureaucracy of a service that is hard to use, and do it more quickly or cheaply than a user would be able to do themselves.

If you look for them, the world is full of services like this – personal accountants, wealth managers and conveyancers are some of the more long-standing and well-known, so much so that we almost forget that we wouldn't need services like this if buying a home or paying tax were simpler.

But in recent years a new generation of 'parasitic services' have evolved to help us negotiate some of the more cumbersome and difficult to understand services. And they're evolving at a surprising rate. Industries that are traditionally hard to negotiate are among the most colonised, with perhaps chief among them being financial services.

UK startup Cleo (which we looked at briefly in principle 4) is a perfect example of this. As a chatbot-based service that sits on top of your many bank accounts, it allows users to manage their finances without interacting with their bank, whose digital services are often clunky and inaccessible, to say of being siloed from one another.

Many of these 'parasitic' services charge users for their time, or the service provider for their service, increasing the cost of the service. These costs are sometimes more efficient than the service provider doing it themselves but this often means that these services eventually exclude users who can't afford to pay to use this service.

There is an entire industry of these services that do just this on behalf of governments around the world. Search 'visa', 'driving licence' or 'passport services' and you will no doubt find one of the many (mostly unsanctioned or fraudulent) services charging users to access what should be a free (or run at cost) public service.

Despite the best efforts of many governments to have these sites removed from search results, these services succeed because a large proportion of digital public services are still only findable and usable by those who are already experts. Services like this are more than happy to take your money in return for their expert mediation of the bureaucracy on your behalf.

Those who don't have the money to pay for one of these services have to invest their time in learning how to negotiate the complexity themselves. Either way the outcome is the same – a service that is only usable by a small group of self-taught experts, or a narrow set of professionals working on behalf of clients who can afford to pay.

This is of course a vicious cycle, with an increasing number of these professionals invested in keeping these services as complex as possible so that they can retain their business model. It often leads to a situation where – because their service has been so complex for so long – the services that these parasitic services live off start to believe that their users are these 'experts' or 'professionals' themselves.

It's particularly prevalent in the public sector, where there are many services who believe their users to be brokers, conveyancers, tax specialists or legal advisors, but this can just as easily happen in the private sector where many – often large and old – providers all work in the same way as each other, forgetting that this isn't intuitive to users. This attitude is caused by an expectation that, because of the ubiquitousness of some services – like getting a pension or finding a new energy supplier – that all users will have a knowledge of how things are done and that they turn to specialists to do this for them 'because it's just easier'. Generally, the more ubiquitous the service, the more expectant we become, and the more complacent of bad design and the more parasitic services there will be.

Even services which are for so-called 'professionals' – that is, people who may do something repeatedly like filing other people's tax returns or helping people to change the name on a government record when they buy a house, will have to have been used by someone who was new to the profession at some point.

It might seem obvious, but no one is born with an innate understanding of how to learn to drive, or what a pension is and why we need one. We generally learn these things from the people around us, but this is a big presumption to make.

It's not just knowledge of how a particular service works specifically that we expect from users, there's also an expectation of something deeper – a bureaucratic literacy that extends to how we interact with even the most simple of situations.

There is no service that will be used just by people who have used it before

Knowing to wait at the entrance to certain restaurants to be seated is an example of this, as is knowing that if you want to get something done in a European healthcare context you have to push for it proactively. These subtle nuances of 'the way things work' are only obvious once they're learned, and are not learned by all.

In 2000, Steve Krug wrote the now infamous book on interaction design 'Don't Make Me Think', which defined how and why we should focus on making our interactions with users as easy as possible.

In it, Krug says: 'If you can't make something self-evident, you at least need to make it self-explanatory... It doesn't matter how many times I have to click, as long as each click is a mindless, unambiguous choice'.

But the ability of your service to be used effectively by someone who has no prior knowledge of it requires more than just simple usability. The experience a first-time user has of your service extends well beyond the moment they actually use your service.

When designing a service that can be used by someone with no prior knowledge of either our service or one like ours, we need to think about:

1   How does someone know your service exists when they need it?
    Does your user know your service exists?

2   How do they find it once they know it's there?
    Can they find it using their own logical searches for what they're looking for?

3   How do they access and use it?
    Does the service clearly explain what it does? Does the user know what to expect, and what is expected of them?

A large part of designing a service for someone who has no prior knowledge of that service comes down to understanding the expectations they have when they use your service, as we saw in principle 3. However, many of these assumptions can be wrong, or lead your user to use your service incorrectly.

Our understanding of a new service is based on past experiences

The habit some people have of hoarding receipts is a perfect example of this. A study conducted by Visa in 2012 revealed that as many as one in 5 of us won't throw away receipts immediately after we're given them. Not because they are useful to us (how many times have you asked for a refund on a meal in a restaurant the next day?) but because we're worried that they contain some kind of usable information that would allow someone to defraud us. Several participants in the study even kept their receipts in bags, envelopes and piles for months, for fear that they might fall into the wrong hands. It's not clear what information is contained on a receipt, and what it might be used for. For many, this means that they automatically leap to the worst possible outcome – that the information contained on a receipt could make the account susceptible to fraud.

When we don't know how a service works, our presumptions of safety, means of access and usability are often based on little more than superstition and presumption. That can lead users to distrust your service when they should trust it, but it can also lead users to do the reverse.

In 2009, before the days of Uber and other ride-hailing apps were prolific, Transport for London (TfL) published an advert warning of the dangers of unbooked minicabs on London's Underground that read 'if your cab's not booked, you're just getting into a stranger's car'.

There had been a spate of attacks on passengers in the few months preceding and TfL came up with the campaign as a way of explaining the dangers of getting into an unknown vehicle. The assumption that your car is not a stranger's car when it's pre-booked however, relies upon a presumption that the driver of your cab works for a company, and that this company presumably keeps some kind of accurate database of its employees so, should something happen, this person would be traceable. This may well be true, but it could just as easily not be true.

It's easy to see just how fragile these beliefs and superstitions are, and how much they affect our interaction with the world on a profound level.

The UK Passport Office found this out when it took the process of applying for a passport from a clunky paper form to a digital service that could be used to renew all adult UK passports

When people don't know how something works, they make it up

online. The team encountered a problem with their new service – and that was that their users were so used to things going wrong with the paper version of the service, they had started to rely on recorded postal delivery as a way of assuring that their application was received. There was no such proof available for the digital service, so many otherwise-completely rational and digitally savvy users resorted to the paper service for 'security'.

What our habit of hoarding receipts, trusting a pre-booked minicab and posting paper passport applications tells us is that no user will arrive at your service with a fresh and unblemished understanding of it.

Your users may be first-time users, but they will come to your service with a set of assumptions, expectations and even superstitions that will need to be corrected, adjusted or reinforced, depending on their accuracy. The first step towards this will be to understand what expectations your users have in the first place. This will mean doing user research to find out.

Once you know and understand the expectations, there will be some that you need to actively contradict, and those you need to design into your service. Only you can know what these are, but as a general rule of thumb try to consider what expectations are good for your users, your company and society at large. If they aren't, they will need to be something you proactively change.

Alongside navigating your user's expectations of your service on first use, you will need to understand how expectations affect other services across the whole user journey.

In order to make your service usable without prior knowledge, it's also good to:

Make sure your service is findable
This means understanding when and how a user might look for support and what language they use to look for it.
For more details, see principle 1

Clearly explain what your service is for
Someone with no knowledge of your organisation or service is still likely to have a clear idea of what they need when they use your service. Your service will need to quickly explain what it is to your user and how it will help them achieve what they're looking to do.
For more details, see principle 2

Make no presumptions about how much your user knows
Do not presume any knowledge or experience of either your service or services like it. Conduct a thorough review to see if there are any presumptions in your service. Make a list of these and work out how many you need to change or, if you can't change, explain them to your users.

Work in a way that's familiar
There will be some ways of working that will be so ubiquitous that to step outside of them would cause confusion. You will only be able to tell which are which by doing enough user research with a diverse group to know which ones 'most people' understand.
For more details, see principle 5

Work in a way that's agnostic to organisational structures
Navigating organisational structures while trying to understand your service can be one of the most difficult things for users with no prior experience of your service to do as it requires a level of orientation, while trying to get to their destination. Somewhat like using a new type of map for each journey.

Make sure your service can be used without knowing or understanding who is providing it.
For more details, see principle 7

7

A good service is agnostic to organisational structures

The service must work in a way that does not unnecessarily expose a user to the internal structures of the organisation providing the service.

In 2016, British company Thriva was founded to enable users to check their health in the safety and comfort of their own home. The service enabled discreet, at-home blood tests for a number of different conditions – including diabetes, hormone imbalances and malnutrition. However, although the service itself has changed the way that health monitoring works for its many users, it's also done something far more interesting.

Alongside being a new way to check your health, Thriva is made up of different component parts, provided by different organisations. Most notably, the service uses the nationwide network of British County Pathology Labs – a group of National Health Service (NHS) testing facilities that can test for anything from cancer to cholesterol. These are the same labs used by NHS hospitals and they have their own rules and regulations around use. All samples must be sent in a strictly labelled format, and shouldn't be sent on a weekend (when the labs are closed). All of these rules have been integrated into the service Thriva provides to enable users to use it.

The fact that this service is provided by multiple organisations, strung together to form one seamless service, is a huge achievement of alignment and collaboration, but this is sadly not the norm for services that cross organisational boundaries, as many do today.

Services in the internet age don't obey organisational boundaries. In a world where users hit Google looking for a service that meets their needs, our services are defined by what our users want to achieve, not by the limits of what we, or any other organisation provides.

As we've seen in principles 1 and 3, where your user starts, and what they expect to find, depends a lot on the level of familiarity your user has with the task they're trying to complete. One rule rings true for all users, regardless of their level of experience – getting something done is always more important than who is providing the service.

When we define our services in this way – by what a user is trying to achieve, not by the boundaries of what we provide – our services will more than likely stretch across multiple organisational boundaries, posing new and complex challenges on the way we run our organisations.

Services in the internet age don't obey organisational boundaries

Take our example of buying a house. When buying a house, we might expect our users to look for a house surveyor, but they may just as easily look for something that will help them to 'buy a house', expecting to find a seamless journey of every step, from reviewing properties to moving in, all in perfect alignment. Our challenge in this situation is to provide a service that helps a user get to their goal, regardless of whether or not that goal is entirely within our current remit to meet.

As we've seen in the introduction to this book, the services that most pre-internet organisations provide simply weren't designed to work in this way, making them hard to find, segmented and siloed. But if our services were not designed for the internet, it is only because the organisations that provide those services weren't set up to deliver services in this way.

Our organisations were designed for a world where a service was devised, then delivered, consistently, with minimal changes for a long period of time. They were designed to be operated in an environment where the pace of change was a lot slower than it is today. These unchanging services were designed to be provided by organisations that also didn't change. After all, software and systems were expensive to build, and skills were difficult to acquire and manage. Instead we designed our businesses around what technology at the time was able to do, not what our users needed, leading us to create organisations that are rigidly structured around a very specific set of tasks.

These tasks tend to be highly specialised at completing one specific part of an end-to-end journey because, ultimately, the more variety to your business, the more complex and variable your systems and software need to be. In a world where your systems are expensive to change, the more specialised you are, the cheaper you become.

An estate agent, for example, has specialist skills and needs access to very different software than the surveyor who makes sure your home is safe to buy. However, this is not the way that services work now – our users expect to know what they're buying, how safe it is and whether they're able to build on it, all at the same time.

Software for commodified businesses like property management are now easy to buy, as are the HR and finance management processes that underpin a multiskilled organisation. Access to skilled workers is also a lot easier than it was, with a job market that now has 20% more university graduates that it did in the 1970s.

For the first time, we are facing unprecedented demands to join up our services that finally match our ability to do something about it. Providing these joined-up services poses a number of challenges that go beyond what skills we have or what software we use though,

There are four fundamental ways our services are designed that cause siloed, fragmented journeys, despite our ability to join those up across organisational boundaries.

Separation of data

The most common reason for a siloed experience of a service is when data about a user isn't shared with the people who need it. This often leads a user to have to give that data to multiple parts of your organisation or across multiple organisations.

Sometimes it is important that this data is separated. For example, the government probably holds more detailed (and meaningful) data on you than any other single organisation. Information like your health records, your criminal record, your marital status and your financial situation. Put these pieces of data into the hands of one person and you could easily rule out of the prospect of employment for some people, based on their medical records or similar.

Sometimes we use a separation between organisations to create these bricks-and-mortar data controls to ensure users are treated well. However, in the majority of circumstances, this separation of data is entirely unconscious. To avoid this, review what data flows through your end-to-end service, who collects it and who has access to it. Try to spot places where the same data is collected multiple times and not shared and design your end-to-end service starting with the data, rather than as an afterthought.

Incompatible processes

Another common area that causes misalignment between steps in a service is when the processes or policies of one organisation don't match up to another. This can be one part of a journey that takes a certain amount of time, and doesn't match up with the deadlines of another, or where we require something from one part of a service journey to continue to the next phase that isn't provided.

Try to look at the requirements that each stage of a service has and look for areas where there is misalignment – what activities do your users have to do, and when do they have to complete these things? Do all of your timelines match up?

Incompatible criteria of use

Slightly less common, though still hugely frustrating for users, is when one part of a service has a set of criteria that means that it can or cannot be used by some people, while other parts of that service use a completely different set of rules.

Try to map out all of the mandatory requirements in your service and see if these are consistent across all touchpoints.

Inconsistent language

Inconsistent language between different organisations or parts of an organisation might seem like a minor issue, but when it comes to asking users to reference certain documents or artefacts that they might need to continue a process, not sharing the same definitions between parts of your service can be hugely disorientating.

Take a look at all of the nouns in your service – documents, processes, activities or things that a user needs to do – and look at how they're referred to in different areas of your service. Create a taxonomy of the things a user might need to refer to and make sure that these are the same in all areas of your service.

Looking at these four areas will help you fix the immediate siloes and breaks in your service, however, it's important to understand why these separations in organisations (or areas within an organisation) exist in the first place so that they don't happen again.

In 1967, Melvin Conway submitted a paper to the *Harvard Business Review* called 'How Do Committees Invent?' It was the first time anyone had explained the phenomena of why siloed organisations produces siloed services. In it, Conway proposed a theory that the structure of an organisation has a direct effect on the structure of the services it provides.

Conway said that if an organisation was made up of separated, isolated software engineers, then they were likely to produce separate, isolated services as a result. This separation wasn't a problem, he said, so long as the designers of each of these pieces of software were able to communicate effectively with each other. This was because: 'each piece of software cannot interface correctly with each other unless the designer and implementer of one piece of software communicates with the designer and implementer of another'. Crucially, this meant that 'the structure of a software system necessarily will show a similarity with the social structure of the organisation that produced it.'

When communication breaks down in this way, we can see this almost as a kind of organisational entropy. A well-organised set of information loses shape and meaning and eventually degrades into a kind of chaos the more times it's translated – just as information is mistranslated in the children's 'telephone game'.

Harvard Business Review rejected Conway's paper on the grounds that he had no proof but, more than 50 years later, Conway's law has gone on to become one of the most important theories that explains why siloed organisations produce siloed services.

What's possibly the most damaging aspect of what Conway found was that the gaps between our organisations have a very real effect, not just in the immediate experience that a user feels, but in our ability to be able to design and deliver a service that meets their needs over time.

Conway said that: 'because the design that occurs first is almost never the best possible, the prevailing system or concept may need to change. Therefore, flexibility of organization is important to effective design.'

The organisation you build is the machine you use to build a service. Just like any other machine or tooling, if it doesn't work properly, or isn't designed well, it won't be able to build the thing it's designed to build.

One of the ways we got over the fact that our organisation might not be the right size or shape to provide a complete end-to-end experience for our users in the past was by merging with or

Siloed organisations produce siloed services

buying the organisations that were involved in providing the same service as us. The two most common models are vertical and horizontal integration.

Vertical integration is where a business expands to the stages of production before or after it. For example, a brick factory that buys a distribution warehouse so it can better store and sell its bricks.

Horizontal integration is where a company buys other companies that do the same thing, so that it can use its tools at a greater scale. A brick factory buys another brick factory.

However, these are economic models designed for product manufacture and don't describe how services like Thriva are integrating with companies that provide other parts of their service.

We're seeing a new economic model emerging, one where a company buys, or makes use of, another company to provide a whole experience for a user – we can think of this as a kind of experience integration.

Experience integration means that you provide an experience across multiple organisations that is integrated. If another company does this and integrates your service into their own, it can mean that your service or organisation needs to take on a very different shape. Switching from being a user-facing service to something altogether more infrastructural, where one service provider provides an end-to-end service service out of component parts found elsewhere on the market.

The new paradigm of 'service aggregators' are a great example of this – where comparison sites like GoCompare, Compare The Market and other similar services make it easy to select and choose from many similar services – for example, electricity suppliers.

Thanks to new smart energy meters, these companies are now extending further into the user journey by enabling users to dynamically switch to a better energy supplier when their rates are preferable, in real time, essentially rendering the services that they are 'comparing' as pure infrastructure.

Similar shifts are also taking place in banking, where services like Plum and Cleo (as we've seen before) sit alongside a host of other friendly banking Facebook chatbots that will help you to navigate the confusing world of accessing your bank account online and moving savings between several banks. In this world, an energy supplier or bank that was at one point in total control of its service and user experience is now beholden to another company as an infrastructure provider.

What each of these examples has in common is that the organisation doing the service integration is, for the first time, doing this while the other organisations remain untouched, often unaware of what has happened. They work because the value they bring to users is that they provide a layer of collaboration between different, previously siloed organisations that would be unachievable by any of the individual organisations on their own.

Experience integration can happen to your service whether you like it or not, and can shift your business model overnight, forcing your previously consumer-facing business into becoming the infrastructure that supports someone else's service. This is market disruption in its purest form. But there is another way.

What these examples and Conway's law show is that, above anything else, communication is the one thing that either makes or breaks your service's ability to provide something that works for your user.

Rather than looking at the ways we can collaborate and work together better, we fixate on getting the perfect structure that will allow everything to work perfectly with minimal crossover. This often results in a proliferation of separate business units, organisations and sub-brands to deliver parts of our service 'efficiently', when what we are really doing is sacrificing communication across the whole journey for a marginally easier way of delivering a single bit of a service.

Your organisation is not just the machine you need to build your service, but the machine you use to repair it when it breaks and design an entirely new service when no one wants to buy the old one. This is a hugely complex set of systems and variables and it is almost impossible to design perfectly. Even if you did, your organisational structure would need to be different tomorrow than it was today.

It's because of this that most organisations are now in a constant state of reorganisation to achieve this mythical perfection, when in reality the most important factor, as Conway says, is to communicate effectively, regardless of your structure. So, how do you make sure your service works across organisational boundaries?

Collaboration is the new target operating model

The answer is that collaboration is a privilege; not everyone has it. If collaboration was easy, we'd all be doing it. The reality is that it's very hard to start, and even harder to continue.

People in different parts of an organisation, or other organisations altogether, work at a different pace, have different objectives and sometimes even financial incentives that mean that they are often at odds with one another.

It's important to remember that the ability to step outside of your day job, and to speak to someone who you aren't directly connected with requires permission, sometimes explicit, sometimes implicit, from the organisation you work within. This permission is a privilege that is not afforded to everyone in your organisation equally.

When enabling collaboration and communication, there are 4 things you can do to support people to collaborate on one shared service:

1   Permission
    Enabling collaboration often means giving permission –
    or creating a permissive environment – for people to step
    outside of their 'day job' to work together. This might mean
    changing cultural aspects of your organisation, but it also
    might mean changing more infrastructural processes
    or budgeting practices that stand in the way of the people
    in your organisation and elsewhere of working together
    effectively.

2   Shared standards
    It's easy to go overboard when trying to standardise
    practices across a service. Doing so removes permission
    to collaborate and work together and can neutralise any
    efforts you make to enable permission. However, there
    are some things that do need to be established collectively
    to ensure everyone can work together.

3   Shared goals
    For an organisation or set of organisations to move towards
    a streamlined service, a shared sense of what the future
    should look like is vital. You can call this what you like – vision,

purpose – but the most important aspect to this is that it's something that everyone in your organisation or organisations were involved in creating and can get behind fully.

4   Shared incentives
For this to work, these shared goals need to be encoded in shared financial incentives. This doesn't just mean key performance indicators (KPIs), but profit-sharing agreements, cost codes and cross charging all need to work smoothly so that money doesn't become a stronger tide than communication, as it can so often be.

In summary

1   Recognise the potential silos in your organisation – or with other organisations that might be providing parts of the same service.
2   If you can't change your operating model, change the way you communicate and collaborate.
3   Consider things that create a permissive environment for collaboration, like shared standards, goals and incentives, to help people work together.

8

A good service requires as few steps as possible to complete

A good service requires as minimal interaction from a user as possible to complete the outcome that they're trying to achieve. Sometimes this will mean proactively meeting a user's needs without them instigating an interaction with your organisation. This may mean occasionally slowing the progress of a service in order to help a user absorb information or make an important decision without having to contact you to help them.

Services are made of small pieces, but they are more than the sum of their parts. How many steps your service has and how quickly your user goes through them is often as important as what those parts do.

The service of buying a house will be broken down into a number of steps, like getting a survey done, that will then be broken down into a number of tasks, like booking the survey to happen and and acting on the results – but have we ever stopped to think about why some of these steps exist as separate activities? Compared to the other areas of service design, we generally spend very little time thinking about how many steps a service needs to have and how quickly a user should move through them. This is partly a result of the fact that most services aren't created from scratch, so we rarely get to question something as fundamental as the number and pace of steps in a service. Instead we see it as the product of accidents and evolution, rather than a conscious choice.

Technical requirements, policy or legal constraints or simply the fact that everyone else does it a certain way are so pervasive within our organisations that we forget that the number and pace of the steps within your service can be designed in a way that best suits what your user wants to achieve, rather than just evolving from the conditions they're in. But before we do this, we first need to understand why those steps are there in the first place.

If a service is something that helps someone to do something, users will want to get to that 'thing' as efficiently as possible. Regardless of whether that thing is something enjoyable like going on holiday or something less enjoyable like paying your taxes. In both cases, you either want to be on holiday, or have finished paying tax in as efficient a way as possible.

It's easy to see all steps within a service as annoying hassles; bits of a broken process that could be eliminated altogether. We dream of a bright shiny future where everything is done for us, and delivered without us even having to ask. Or do we? Every new step in your service is a transitional moment. The difference between choosing something and buying it, or between buying and returning something.

When thinking about how many steps your service needs, there is a simple rule: the number of steps in your service should be equal to the number of decisions your user has to make, no more and no less.

A good rule of thumb is to think to yourself – if this thing was done automatically without my knowing about it, would that be a good thing? If the answer is no, then it's best to create a separate step to your service to make sure that your user has full visibility and control over what they're doing. Separate steps in your service also give important moments of transparency on what you as a service provider are doing.

Don't just design the steps of your service, design the space between them

As much as these steps should be designed, the 'empty space' between them is something to be designed too. If used correctly, these transitional moments aren't just empty spaces, but spaces with purpose – to give users visibility and control of a decision they need to make to move forward with their goal.

Japanese dry landscape gardens capture this idea perfectly. Often called 'zen gardens', they are comprised of very few elements spaced out over a large distance. Often just a small mound of moss or stone, surrounded by a sea of gravel, these gardens are built on the principle of '*yohaku no bi*' or the beauty of white space. Graphic designers have used this principle for years, spending just as much time looking at the space between the words, paragraphs, images or pictures they're designing with as they do on the thing themselves, but the same is true of services.

Just as in a traditional zen garden, the space between steps in a service serves a useful function in its own right to highlight the importance of the things around it.

Each break in a service gives us time to reflect on the next thing we have to do. These spaces are an opportunity to pause, to think and decide what route to take next. However, it's often easy for us to decide what pace our users need to go through our service without real consideration of their needs. In 2014 the UK government brought in a piece of legislation called the Consumer Contracts Regulations that did just this.

The legislation stipulated that when a user switches between insurers, utility or broadband suppliers, there must be a mandatory 14 day 'cooling-off' period, where a user can cancel their contract without facing any charges. In order to enforce this, it also stipulated that the user shouldn't receive any contact from their new supplier in that time.

The legislation was created in part because sites like uSwitch, GoCompare, Compare The Market and others had made it so fast and seamless to help users to switch suppliers. The UK government felt that users were being forced into making a decision about a new supplier too quickly, then being faced with hefty penalty charges for terminating their contracts when they changed their minds. While this sounds like a great idea in principle, stipulating a cooling-off period after someone has been forced to make a decision too quickly is the service design equivalent to a sticking plaster on a broken leg.

Energy and broadband providers saw their complaints go through the roof because their services often involve installation or physical checks of equipment in a user's home for the service to start. Waiting 14 days with no word from your new supplier made users understandably confused and nervous.

What this story tells us is that where you place breaks in your service for additional decision-making is almost as important as putting them there in the first place. Rather than solving the issue of being signed up too quickly with no pauses for deliberation, this piece of legislation inserted a pause after a decision had already been made that served to thoroughly confuse users.

How many steps there need to be in your service isn't the only deciding factor that will allow you to design the right 'composition' of parts for your user. Just like a piece of music, your service should have a certain rhythm to the number of steps, but there's a tempo or speed to those things that will vary between services (depending on what's appropriate).

Some services might have relatively few steps, but need to be slowed down – either to allow for decision-making, for example, during treatment for a complex illness, or for a user to experience something they might enjoy, like checking into a luxury hotel.

When designing a service it's important not to just think about what steps you have in your but rhythm of those steps (how many steps there are) and the tempo of your service (how quickly those steps need to happen in succession to one another).

Rhythm

How many steps there are in your service
Use the number of steps according to how many decisions a user has to make.

Tempo

How fast this series of steps is put into action
Use the speed of those steps to adjust for the fact that a decision might be big – and require more thinking space – or relatively minor and require less.

Use tempo in your service to also respond to situations where decisions don't necessarily need to be made, but where a user's attention needs to be focused on something more fully – for example, experiencing something they might enjoy.

Every service is different. How fast your user needs to complete something, how many decisions they need to make along the way, and how much time they need to think will dictate how long and how complex a service needs to be. Only user research will help you find this out, but generally speaking it's helpful to think about two types of service.

However, it's useful to think about the number of steps and the pacing between them as a kind of spectrum that stretches from services that are more involved and require lots of decisions or time to think and focus, and faster services that are more transactional, with fewer steps.

Involved services

These services tend to happen where either more time, consideration or mindfulness is called for, so they tend to have more or slower steps.

Medical services are a great example of this, where treatment might need to be made quickly, but time and consideration need to be made over the types of choices available to patients.

Transactional services

Transactional services are services that need to be done very quickly with as little interaction as possible – paying your taxes or buying groceries, for example. They tend to have fewer or faster steps.

Highly commercial services often try to become more transactional in order to actively reduce the decision-making involved in a buying situation. Amazon's one-click ordering button that can be preprogrammed to order any number of household items is a good example of this.

There is a wide spectrum between a 'transactional' and 'involved' service.

Equally, services can have both transactional and involved parts. For example, when going on holiday, you might want the booking process to be quick and transactional, but the process of arriving for your flight and being welcomed by staff to be more supportive and involved.

Deciding how many steps your service needs and how fast they need to be will mean stepping outside of the reality of your existing service more than any other change you can make to your service.

You might not be able to construct your service perfectly according to what your users need straight away, but by understanding where the decision points lie within your service,

and how major those decisions are, you can start to understand where steps might need to be merged or separated in future.

In summary

1   **Review where decisions need to be made in your service**
     Look at your service from end to end and identify the
     decisions a user needs to make. If there isn't an existing
     step, consider making one. If you have too many steps,
     look to where you can merge these into fewer steps to
     make the journey simpler for your user.

2   **Allow users to focus on one task at a time**
     Users need to be able to focus in order to make a decision.
     Look at areas of your service where multiple decisions
     have been merged into one step and consider breaking
     these down into more steps.

3   **Think about how fast or slow your steps need to be**
     Look at how big the decisions in your service are, or where
     your user might need to be more focused and 'present in
     the moment' to experience something. Consider slowing
     these areas down and, likewise, speeding up areas where
     decisions are minor.

9

A good service is consistent throughout

The service should look and feel like one service throughout, regardless of the channel it is delivered through. The language used should be consistent, as should visual styles and interaction patterns.

When Ajax Football Club made it to the European Cup Final in 1969, everyone was surprised. As a small team from Amsterdam, they'd had mixed success. They'd been founding members of the Netherlands' first professional football league in the 1950s but since then they'd struggled to make an impact on an international level, until in 1965 when they decided to try something new. That something new was an ex-player and relatively unknown manager from the outskirts of Amsterdam, by the name of Rinus Michels, and Michels had some new ideas. After spending 12 years as a player for Ajax, and a few years coaching smaller regional teams, he'd been inspired to try a new method of coaching his teams, where players took up any position they liked on the pitch.

Rather than a formation where each player plays a preset position, meaning that they stick to certain areas of the pitch during the match, Michels proposed training his players to play flexibly, making sure each player could take up any position at any time during the match. Even the goalkeeper, he said, shouldn't be confined to the goal.

The team trained in the new method for months, and when they stepped out onto the pitch in Germany, no one expected them to win. Newspapers had received tip-offs about Michels' radical plan and predicted what would surely be a disaster – after all, how can anyone play properly if they don't know whether they're supposed to be scoring goals or stopping the other side's goals from being scored? However, not only were Ajax able to work out who should be scoring and who shouldn't, but they were able to take opportunities a more structured team wouldn't. Any player in the right position could press forward with the ball if they managed to get it, and score.

Ajax played valiantly, although they were ultimately beaten by Milan, but there was no going back. By the time the whistle blew at 90 minutes, the face of football had changed forever, and Totaalvoetbal (or Total Football) as Michels later called it was born.

What Michels understood about football was something that would take another 40 years for statisticians David Sally and Chris Anderson to define in The Numbers Game – that football is a weak link sport.

In football, you will almost never see one person dribble the ball from one end of the field to another – a lot of players have to touch the ball to make a goal. Every goal is the sum effort of multiple players keeping the ball from the opposition, and passing it up the pitch so that it can be kicked into the goal – one weak link in that process provides an opportunity for the other team get possession of the ball and score. That means a football team is only as strong as the weakest player – the person who misses that crucial pass before a goal, or loses the ball to the other team on the way. Football – unlike basketball, where teams can rely on one or two superstar player to score throughout the game – is a weak link sport.

But a weak link game is also highly unpredictable. Having so many passes and touches to the ball means that at any moment the game can change dramatically. Michels understood this, and trained every player in his team to be as strong as each other, regardless of the circumstances or what position they played. Ajax won every match because, unlike other teams, there were no weak links in their team under any circumstances.

But it's not just in sport that the idea of 'weak links' explains why things that involve multiple people delivering an outcome either succeed or fail. The theory was used in economics by Charles Jones to describe why certain developing countries remain less economically successful, despite investment into specific economy-boosting industries like manufacture and roads.

Jones' theory is that, although countries like Ethiopia or the Democratic Republic of Congo have spent billions on improving industry, these industries aren't as successful as their counterparts in more developed countries because of a lack of all the other supporting elements that make those industries thrive.

A clothing manufacturer in Addis Ababa, for example, will not just need cotton to make their clothes, but clean water to wash them, power to run their sewing machines, roads to move goods in and out, and a skilled workforce to manage the work – to say nothing of a thriving sales network.

Any situation that relies on the work of multiple people to deliver something can be understood as a kind of chain, with weaker and stronger parts that add up to overall success or failure. One weak link in this chain, and a business doesn't thrive as much as its competitors in other markets that have access to these things.

As we've seen in principles 4 and 7, services are made up of many different parts, often delivered by many different partners.

If each of these links is strong, they mesh together as one seamless, coherent experience. Get it wrong, though, and your user is exposed to a gap that either means they can't continue with your service, or don't feel comfortable doing so. Unlike football, where you get as many chances as you can make in 90 minutes to score, you have just one attempt at making a service experience seamless for your user.

These gaps in services can come in many forms – with the most common being inconsistency between steps in the service. This often happens where effort has been put into one part of a service, but not another, such as a ticket booking service where the process of buying the ticket is great, but finding your ticket when you need it is impossible.

British company Trainline – which helps users to book and use train tickets on any train in Europe – recently realised this when it discovered, despite making the booking process incredibly easy across multiple providers – the email address that sent confirmation emails wasn't semantically findable within most people's inboxes as 'trainline', meaning that the service failed in the moments just before a user went to collect their tickets from a ticket machine.

Thankfully, Trainline realised this in research and worked to change the address that sent its confirmation emails. Beyond this it also spent the next couple of years with ticket producers to ensure that tickets could be issued digitally to fix the problem of searching for an email altogether.

Another common area of inconsistency in services is in the experience that users have of a service on different channels. This can happen for a number of reasons, but by far the most common is that one area of a service is more heavily invested in than the others – often resulting in an experience that has been well-designed in its digital form, but hasn't been communicated as a process or set of values to the rest of the organisation – be that over the phone or face-to-face.

British supermarket Tesco is a perfect example of this. As an organisation founded in 1919, which boomed in the 1960s under founder Jack Cohen's motto of 'pile it high and sell it cheap', Tesco has weathered the transition to digital grocery shopping better than most, with profits of £2.21 billion and a share of 27% of the UK grocery market in 2019.

The most recent iteration of its development has been to widen the scope of people who can use their services by expanding the gendered honorifics the digital service used, from simply accepting Mr, Mrs, Miss and Ms to include Mx – a gender-neutral honorific used by people who are nonbinary or agender (ie, they don't identify as either a man or a woman). This was a move that closely followed many banks and high-street retailers in the UK, which began to introduce nonbinary titles as early as 2014.

This company stance to support trans and nonbinary people is well integrated into the digital experience, and clearly supported by an engaged digital team. However, if a customer happens to wander off the digital pathway, their experience soon changes.

One customer, having received a phone call that their delivery was going to be late was addressed by a (clearly confused) customer support operator on the phone who, unable to pronounce 'Mx' asked: 'Hello, is that errrr... umm... Mrs Brown?' It was no doubt a serious undertaking for the digital team to introduce Mx into the honorifics it uses – most customer record systems are sadly still outsourced and require significant development to change. However, whatever effort the team put into ensuring the digital experience was consistent for nonbinary users, was soon revealed to be inconsistent to the company as a whole, given that no one had trained the call centre staff to pronounce it. This particular customer also received several letters after that call, all addressed, as the operator had identified them, as 'Mrs Brown' – showing how these inconsistencies can sometimes replicate elsewhere if not identified and stopped. What this weak link in the Tesco shopping service revealed is an inconsistency of company policy to respect the identities of nonbinary individuals.

A change made by a digital team, probably without the knowledge of the rest of the organisation, wasn't simply a change to functionality but a policy change that needed to be applied consistently across all parts of the service. The fact that it wasn't made it clear that this was far from a universally held policy, and has lead to mistrust of the brand among the trans and nonbinary community.

In essence, what sits behind this inconsistency of user experience is an inconsistency in the way that the teams who provide these services work – just as Michels discovered in football.

These weak links within organisations can have dramatic effects, particularly if that service is delivered entirely by people.

A tragic example of this is the story of Victoria Climbié, an 8-year-old girl who lived in Haringey in London, who sadly died as the result of abuse.

Abuse is all too often missed by local authorities. What was unusual about Victoria's story was that she was known to four different local authorities in London – including many social workers, housing officers, paediatricians and the National Society for the Prevention of Cruelty to Children (NSPCC).

There are many reasons why a case like this fails to make its way successfully through a system, however, in this case a large contributor to Victoria falling through the cracks was that no one person in the system of care that surrounded her was trained to spot both physical injuries and signs of abuse, while also being empowered to do something about that problem. Each individual was trained in their own specialism, but no one individual had a holistic view of Victoria's story, an inquiry revealed.

What the story of Victoria Climbié and nonbinary customers of Tesco reveal is that it is inconsistencies in the ways in the way people work on services that cause inconsistencies in the services themselves, whether that's an inconsistency between individuals across organisations in charge of care, or between different groups within one organisation – digital and phone.

Neither Tesco nor Haringey Council developed the rounded skills of staff so that they understand the service they're providing consistently. Instead they focused on a few elite specialists, creating weak links in their teams as a whole.

Though completely different services, what they share is an example of what happens when a strength held in one area isn't consistently shared across an organisation. Whether this is an ability to identify abuse, understand what nonbinary gender is, or the ability to both stop and score goals, sharing perspectives and ideas equally across organisations is the thing that enables us to respond to a quickly to changes in circumstances and deliver consistently. Every time.

All of these examples lead us to the question – if we are aware that the failures in our services are the fault of weak links in the way we work as a team, why do we persist in thinking about protecting or growing our stronger links when situations like this happen?

Again, we can turn to football for an answer: 'I try to advise the oligarchs that own teams that they would be better off spending their 80 million on four pretty good players, rather than one super-star player but they don't listen,' David Sally said, after publishing The Numbers Game. 'But oligarchs don't just buy teams to win matches, they buy them for lots of different reasons including hanging out with good-looking players and selling lots of shirts. A weak link strategy just isn't as glamorous.'

It turns out we don't value the weak links because they aren't the superheroes. Having another Lionel Messi or Abby Wambach on our team gets us kudos and support in a way that training a full squad to be solid players never would.

The same is true of services, where we will often focus on one superstar part of our service over and above any other element. Whether this is the account creation, booking or reviewing your details part of the service, we often justify this decision because we think that one moment in a service is more important than any other. In reality, although there are points in a journey where failure has more of an effect than another – being able to complete a service from start to finish is far more important than having a great experience in one moment, then not be able to complete the rest of the journey.

Another reason we justify focusing on these superhero moments is that one part of our service might be developed more easily if it's focused on in isolation to the others. Again, although it's important to prioritise, instead of a minimum viable product, like signing up for a new account – which often leaves our users stranded in on our perfect product with nowhere to go – we need to think about minimum viable service instead.

~~Minimum viable product~~

Minimum viable service

It's not always possible – or wise – to develop an entire service all at once, but there's a big difference between creating a usable service then improving parts of it, and creating a desert-island of a product and expecting your users to swim to it.

When we build a minimum viable service, we should be aiming for a service through which most of our users will navigate to achieve the goal they set out to do. Starting from the point of view of a minimum viable service rather than product forces us to think about which areas need to be in place before your service is usable.

As we've seen in the case of Ajax, Trainline, Tesco and Haringey Council, consistency is a vital part of service design that can only be mastered when we think about how the whole team operates together. However, consistency is very often mistaken as uniformity – where we aim for a service experience that is exactly the same across all parts of the journey, all channels and between different users.

While it's vital for services to be consistent, they are also complex and varied, and some parts of your service will need to look and behave differently from the rest. For example, how you talk to your users when they sign up for an account is different to how you then talk to your users when they have a complaint that needs solving.

Apply the same principles to each part of your service, which might be functionally quite unique, and your service can come across as unresponsive or confusing. This is why it's important for your service to be consistent, but not uniform.

British mobile telecoms company O2 quickly found this out when in 2012, its entire network went down for a period of 24 hours.

This blackout happened relatively early on in the era of universally used mobile internet and, much as the earliest power cuts must have come as a shock to places with previously reliable, infallible electricity, this sudden outage of one of the UK's biggest telecoms companies was met with predictable levels of disappointment. Hundreds of thousands of people were affected, and the complaints came in thick and fast on Twitter and Facebook.

For the first few hours, the O2 social media team followed standard practice: 'We're sorry about the interruption to your service. For the latest service status update visit http://status.o2.co.uk', until one of O2's social media team – a man named Chris – decided to take matters into his own hands.

Instead of the same reply when someone tweeted, 'Not gonna lie cannot wait to leave @O2', Chris replied, 'But we still love you'. And on it went. Customer: 'FUCK YOU! SUCK DICK IN HELL @O2'. Chris: 'Maybe later, got tweets to send right now.'

These responses were risky. It would have been safer for Chris to wait for a party line, but what his responses had that the standard ones didn't was a human voice, dealing with a situation in the best way possible rather than reading from a script. This wouldn't be appropriate for any of the other examples we've just discussed, but the same rules apply. Had anyone complained about either of these situations and received an off-script response the result would almost have been as bad as inconsistency in a situation of crisis.

When users need a solution to a complex problem, it's a human, tailored response that they need, not a scripted bot. But responding and working with a user's individual circumstance with freedom requires empowered staff.

This is something that the US online shoe and clothing brand Zappos understood when hiring customer support operatives. Zappos has a policy of empowering its staff to deal with complaints and returns in whatever way they feel appropriate, meaning that when one customer phoned to say that their husband had died and could they return the shoes, they did just that, and sent flowers too. Another customer, who was late for a wedding, contacted Zappos asking if they had any shoes in his size in his local store. They responded and sent the shoes directly to him by courier that day.

These are the types of examples of 'magical' customer experience we're often given at conferences and in books that espouse the benefits of 'customising' or 'tailoring' our services to users. In reality this isn't about customisation, but a human response that doesn't follow arbitrary rules, or services that are consistent, but not uniform.

It's easy to forget the consistent part of a service when you are focused on not being uniform though. If Chris or another advisor had replied to some O2 customers with the standard response, and others with the new 'human' voice it would have seemed

Good services are consistent, not uniform

unfair, causing far more anger than the original scripted response alone.

This response of perceived unfairness in inconsistent services is a well-recognised one and can be seen in the way people respond to the different grades on airlines. A study by Harvard Business School discovered that the rates of violence on flights rises by 30% when customers have to walk directly through first class to get to economy.

Although it's not always appropriate to deliver the same service to every user, it is important to make your user feel as if the service is fair and to minimise the perceived inconsistency in the service to certain users over others.

It can be hard to find the line between delivering a service that is just consistent enough to not cause weak links in a user's experience, and one that is so uniform and unresponsive to a user's individual circumstances that it feels inhumane. Only you will know exactly where that line lies, however, there are a few things that will help you find where this line is.

When thinking about consistency, think about these four dimensions:

1   Consistency across user journey
    Ensure that when you think about developing your service you think about the minimum viable service, and make a plan to ensure that there are no gaps in your user's journey that have been neglected.

2   Consistency in each channel
    The digital channel might be your main route of interaction with your users, as might your phone or face-to-face service – but your users will interact with your service in multiple ways. Make sure you've tested each channel from start to finish with your journey, and have tested what the transition is between these channels.

3   Consistency over time
    Make sure that changes to your service are equally applied to all channels, parts of the journey and partners involved in providing your service for the duration of your service's

lifespan. One year of neglect to a channel or to a moment in the journey can very often mean that your service develops a weak link. Organise regular reviews to make sure your service is tested from every angle on a regular basis.

4 Consistency between users
You may offer premium versions of your service, but make sure it is clear why you do this. Try to offer an equally human service to all users, not just those who have paid more, and decide which are the basic rights within your service that everyone should receive. Look long and hard at these until they seem inline with the expectations you would have in the rest of your life. For example, most users will understand if you get a better seat or faster broadband if you pay more, but there will be aspects of your service that should be available to all users – like seatbelts and telephone support. Make sure your business model reflects this.

In order to make sure you have consistency, but not uniformity across these different aspects of your service, try to remember the following principles:

1 Every breach of consistency is a breach of trust
When our services behave inconsistently, our reaction is the same as we would react to a person who did the same – mistrust. Just as in the rest of our lives, it's a lot harder to regain that trust once it's broken than it is to gain it in the first place. Treat every weak link with care and consideration and try to avoid breaking your user's trust in you.

2 Focus on the abilities of your whole organisation, not on the skills of your superstar players
Your service is made of multiple partners and individuals, all working towards a common goal. For that team to work together on a service that has no weak links, your team has to be free of weak links.

Make sure everyone in your team knows and understands the skills of everyone else so that they can respond to change quickly. Make sure that vital pieces of information about how a user should experience something is transferred universally across your organisation.

3   **Empower staff to make individual decisions about users**
To make sure that your service doesn't stray into being uniform, ensure that your staff are empowered to make individual decisions about how to respond to users or to fix a problem in the best way they see fit. This applies to treating users differently at all points in your user's journey to respond to their particular needs at the time.

Good services are only as strong as their weakest link

10

A good service should have no dead ends

A service should direct all users to a clear outcome, regardless of whether the user is eligible or suitable to use the service. No user should be left behind or stranded within a service without knowing how to continue.

Picture the scene: you're halfway through using a service and you realise that you've changed the phone number that you used to sign up, you don't have proof of address because you've just moved house or your situation doesn't fit any of the options you've been given by the automatic answering machine when you called up.

We've all been there at some point, but whatever the reason was that got you there, the result is the same: you're stuck with nowhere to go. Your next step? Probably a desperate search for a human being who you can reason with to get out of your seemingly inescapable service cul-de-sac.

This happened to Sarah Blake, like it has to thousands of people, when she left her mobile phone in the back of an Uber on a night out. Realising immediately what she'd done, Sarah tried to contact Uber to get her phone back by using her partner's phone. Unfortunately, the only way to contact the driver was using the app and, after trying to log in using the back-up phone, Sarah realised she had two-factor authentication turned on, meaning that the only way to trace her phone was by using her phone to get into the app.

Sarah was stuck with nowhere to go, when she realised that, even though Uber had accidentally created a dead end in its service, she was able to trace her phone using Apple's 'Find My Phone' app.

After watching her phone being driven around London all night, it eventually came to rest at the home of the unwitting Uber driver in Dagenham – a suburb of the city.

Sarah visited the driver the next morning (who was understandably surprised to see her) and thankfully got her phone back, but her success in achieving her goal was spite of Uber's service, not because of it. Her phone was nearly out of battery by the time the driver finished his shift and, had it died, she'd have had no chance of recovering it. Although Uber's service is designed to be used on a mobile, it hasn't been designed for the scenario where that mobile phone is lost, despite the many people around the world who have no doubt lost their phone in the back of a cab.

All services fail, but these 'dead-end' failures are different. They happen when a user hits a point in your service – either because they don't have access to something, they can't do something or they simply aren't something – where they can't go on any further.

Some of these dead ends will be for legitimate reasons – for example, a person who isn't qualified for a place at a certain university won't be able to get a place at that university. But some happen because we failed to account for a particular situation a user might be in – for example, they might not be able to provide proof of their previous qualifications because they qualified a long time ago.

Not everyone can take the same route to the same outcome within a service and there often needs to be many possible pathways to the same outcome to cater for the types of scenarios your users will find themselves in.

Dead ends happen when someone strays from what we like to call the 'happy path' – either because they can't do something, they don't have access to something or because they aren't someone who can use your service. This happy path is often designed with an imaginary 'ideal' user in mind, but when we design for the 'ideal' user, we are often designing for a person who rarely exists.

People have different abilities, life circumstances and access to information at the time they use your service that mean that at any point, any one of them can veer from this so-called happy path. Dead ends happen when we fail to predict all of the reasons why someone might not be able to do what we've asked them to do within our service, or where we have designed a pathway that is too narrow to accommodate even a minor deviance – for example, a lost credit card.

Dealing with these varying scenarios can seem daunting when you're designing your service, but it doesn't have to be. The first step is to understand the reasons why your user might face a dead end in your service.

There are four main reasons why a user might be faced with a dead end:

1. They're not eligible to use your service

This is the one 'intentional' dead end your user might face – where someone has a situation that simply doesn't fit your service. For example, someone lives too far away for you to deliver to them, or doesn't meet the criteria your service has set out for another reason.

Although your service might not suit them, try to deal with these dead ends as elegantly as possible, providing onward links to relevant support where possible. Just because they aren't able to use your service to reach their end goal doesn't mean your service isn't part of their journey to be able to do this.

All too often, people are excluded from services for reasons that don't make commercial sense or fairness to users, simply because we haven't understood the demand from a particular group. It's a good idea therefore to collect information about why that user was trying to use your service – for example, if your service doesn't cater to people in their area, but you find that there's sufficient demand, you may be able to change this.

2. They've strayed off the beaten track

Sometimes dead ends happen more gradually than simply giving someone no option to continue. Services that are very simple for those on the 'happy path' often hide complex and hard to navigate side routes that don't necessarily 'stop' a user from doing something, but slow them down to the extent that they can't get what they need to do done.

If your service has complex elements further down the route, it's best to explain these at the start, rather than giving users the expectation that your service is simple all the way through. Make sure when you're designing your service that the complexity is

evenly distributed and doesn't come as a surprise when
they wander off the beaten track.

3. They can't do something

It's important to consider the abilities of your users and make
sure you have routes to use your service that are accessible to
everyone. We often expect seemingly simple, easy things from
our users that for some, at some points in their lives, are far from
simple or easy.

You will need to do some user research to find out the barriers
within your particular service, but common ones include:

The ability to remember long numbers
**Long numbers are difficult for anyone, especially those
with dyslexia, dyspraxia and other cognitive difficulties.**

The ability to follow complex instructions
Particularly those with autism and some learning difficulties.

The ability to remember dates, times and appointments
**Difficult for those with dyslexia, dyspraxia and other
cognitive difficulties.**

The ability to get somewhere physically
**Often a struggle for those with physical disabilities, people
who have social anxiety or a lack of a car, access to public
transport or money to pay for either of these.**

The ability to get somewhere or do something during
working hours
**Difficult for most people who work standard office hours,
but more so for those on zero-hours contracts, those working
multiple jobs or those with caring responsibilities.**

The ability to read a language fluently
Difficult not just for non-native speakers of your language,

but often difficult for speakers of international sign languages and those with severe dyslexia.

The ability to read PDFs or access 'non-accessible' digital services
PDFs are often hard to read for users who use a digital screen reader or other assistive technologies. Avoid putting any critical information into a downloadable PDF brochure or similar.

When designing your service, try to think about the different abilities you expect your user to have. List them all – even the ones you think everyone can do – and test these throughout your service. Notice where they have the most effect and try to minimise as many of these as possible. Also, try to avoid any one of these things becoming a 'critical' requirement that your user must be able to do to progress through your service.

4. They don't have access to something

Presuming your user has access to something that makes your service run more smoothly isn't necessarily a problem. What is a problem is where we either expect too many of these things or we rely solely on access to one particular thing without any back-up options. When this happens, the consequences can be catastrophic for users, and seemingly small or temporary dead ends – such as being locked out from your account at a critical moment – can be just as damaging as missing an appointment and might mean you're not able to use a service indefinitely.

Just as you have done with the things you presume your user can do, the first task is to identify all of the things you assume your users will have access to at any given point in their journey, and analyse what happens when they don't have access to these things.

As a rule of thumb, you should try to minimise this list of absolute requirements to as few as possible while ensuring your service is secure. This can be a difficult balance to strike but,

Evenly distribute the complexity

where you have things that you need from your user, consider having back-ups that they might use if they don't have access to the thing that you've asked for. For example, if you need someone to prove their address, think about alternative ways of doing this rather than relying on a bank statement or utility bill.

Below are the most common things most services presume users have ready access to:

- A phone number
- A bank account or credit/debit card
- An email address
- Official identification, such as passport, driving licence or state-issued ID card
- An address, or proof of address
- Any of the above, in the country that you're operating in
- Any unique identifiers your company uses to identify that user, for example, policy numbers, account numbers, booking references

Not having access to these things can happen more commonly than you think. Equally some will link to one another, forming a kind of chain reaction if one isn't accessible. For example, without a phone number many services won't be able to use two-factor authentication, which your service might need to access confidential account information required to verify someone's identity.

However, by far the most common thing we presume users have access to is the internet. This is not surprising, as the ubiquity of the internet has grown – however, it becomes a problem when we rely solely on someone's access to one channel, whatever that channel might be.

Many of our stereotypes about who has and who hasn't got access to the internet are simply wrong. However, much more damaging is our presumption that access to the internet is stable and predictable.

Anyone who has tried to use the internet on public transport can tell you this isn't true. However, it's not just situations where a user is travelling that we need to account for. Loss of income can mean broadband bills don't get paid, loss of a mobile phone or tablet can mean not having access, too. Equally, being abroad with high roaming charges or living in an area with poor reception can have an effect on someone's ability to use the internet.

When we introduced the internet to our means of using services, we presumed it would subsume all other channels in a way that we never expected telephony to do, meaning we often rely on it solely for some of the main functionality of our services – such as identification.

However, when new layers of technology get added to a service, we rarely turn the old ones off. This has the effect that each new technology adds an additional channel to our service where some services might exist as post, phone, face-to-face and chatbot simultaneously. When done well, each new technology is treated as a progressive enhancement on the last, meaning that when a user is unable to access a service using one technology, we can rely on the one that came before it to enable the user to reach their end goal. We can see this as a king of a progressive enhancement in reverse, or a progressive degeneration of the service.

At some point this means that some services will need to operate what we can think of as a 'service of last resort' – where, because a user's circumstance is so complex, the service needs to be performed entirely by a human with nothing but their own judgement.

The 'government diplomatic bag' is a great example of this. Most governments will have some form of this service. It is possibly one of the oldest, and yet least encountered, services many governments provide because its main purpose is to carry government mail to citizens who live in countries and areas that aren't accessible by normal means. Every year, thousands of tax statements, pension cheques, death certificates and other important pieces of mail need to be delivered to people living in areas where the postal system doesn't work. If this is the case, any letters for you from the government will be sent in the diplomatic bag to your nearest embassy. Sometimes the service carries on from here, and occasionally an embassy employee has been known to hand-deliver important pieces of mail themselves.

If this sounds like a service from another century, that's no coincidence. This is the first version of most governments' global

The service of last resort

No user
left behind

postal delivery service. It predates most countries' postal services by a couple of hundred years and is still the last resort when all other methods fail. You can see this as an example of an antiquated system, but this is in fact a brilliant example of how a normally efficient modern service supports users to reach a goal, even when all normal means of support have been exhausted.

In summary, there are six main ways that you can mitigate dead ends in your service:

1   Provide onward routes for people who aren't eligible to use your service

2   Evenly distribute the complexity of your service
Make sure your service doesn't get unduly complex as you stray further from the beaten track.

3   Ensure your service is inclusive
Make sure you understand what you're presuming your users are able to do, and make sure an inability to do one or more of these things isn't a blocker to users being able to complete their goal.

4   Minimise the number of 'requirements' you ask of users
Try to keep the number to things that are absolutely required of users to a minimum to avoid them getting stuck if they can't do them or don't have access to that one thing.

5   Build affordances
Make sure that there are alternative routes for those who can't do something or don't have access to something.

6   Let your service degrade gracefully
Treat each new technology as a progressive enhancement on the last, meaning that, when services fail, you can rely on the technology that came before it.

11

A good service is usable by everyone, equally

The service must be usable by everyone who needs to use it, regardless of their circumstances or abilities. No one should be less able to use the service than anyone else.

Food banks are now a disturbingly common feature of Britain's towns and cities. Used by millions across the country who are unable to afford to feed themselves and their families, they perform a vital role in supporting some of the most vulnerable people in society. The reasons why people need to use food banks are varied, but a significant portion of those who use them are there because of the vicious cycle of increasing difficulty in accessing what they need when their situation worsens.

Linda O'Donnell was one such example. Linda was a fit and healthy care worker, when she was diagnosed with cancer at the age of 57. She couldn't do her previous job because of the time off she needed to go through treatment, so she started to look for more flexible work.

She couldn't find any and eventually applied for government benefits. Linda moved in with her sister so she could get the support she needed, and things looked stable for a while, until Linda needed to go into hospital. She couldn't work any longer, so the benefits she was receiving ran out. She needed to reapply for a different scheme to support her while she was recovering, but the letter asking her to do this went to her old address.

Linda's sister worked as a school administrator and, with 3 children, was struggling to feed the family. It would take a further 6 weeks for Linda to get her new benefits, but the family was running out of money. Linda needed to go for a physical assessment for her new benefits but she didn't have the money to travel by taxi and found the bus too exhausting. Eventually she gave up on getting support and the family turned to a local food bank for help.

Linda's story is tragic but it's not unusual. When thinking about making sure that a service is usable by everyone, we tend to think only about people with physical or cognitive disabilities. But, while making sure that your service is accessible to those with different abilities is hugely important, there are many reasons why certain groups of people might be more likely to be excluded from your service, which are bigger than the scope of what we commonly refer to as 'disabilities'.

Linda was stopped from getting the help she needed because the pathway from 'looking for work' to 'too ill to work' wasn't designed for someone who had poor mobility and couldn't travel, but it also wasn't designed for someone who couldn't afford a taxi, had a changeable address and didn't have a car.

As we saw in principle 10, getting through a service without getting stuck along the way can be challenging for anyone, for any number of reasons. Not being able to use a phone, read complex instructions or visit a physical location during the week is a situation that any of us could find ourselves in at any time in our lives, but these requirements can affect a person who has lost their job, is dyslexic or works long shifts more than most.

These problems frequently cross over, where someone might not be able to do something because of a temporary situation (like a broken arm) or a long-term condition (like an amputation). For example, a user's ability to access your service might be just as restricted by their lack of ability to call you during office hours because they're at work, as it might be if they have autism and find it hard to use the phone. Either way, calling you is going to be hard.

Situations like Linda's and the millions like her happen because we design our services for a world where everyone has permanent 20/20 vision, drop-of-a-pin hearing, a flexible job, plenty of money, stable mental health and a host of other rarely combined superpowers.

In reality, people like this rarely exist and, even if they did, they wouldn't stay like that for long. At any point, this so-called 'normal' user could be sitting in a noisy room holding a baby in one arm, break their arm, lose their job or suffer mental health issues that mean they suddenly, even if temporarily, find themselves outside of this incredibly narrowly defined 'norm' of who can use your service.

Sadly though, it's not just a user's ability to do something – like read, see or make a phone call – that poses a barrier to using a service that hasn't considered the diversity of a person's situation or abilities. All too often, things that are to do with who a person is – such as their gender, sex or religion – are also added to this list of qualities required by services for optimum use.

What we define as 'normal' is hugely affected by the biases of the person creating that definition. Unfortunately because of a lack of diversity in our organisations, we often then find that 'normal' is not just everything we've talked about above, but generally young, white, male, cisgender and heterosexual, too.

There's no such thing as a 'normal' user

These more subtle biases stop users from accessing services just as much as the inability to read a badly formatted PDF, or an inaccessible step into a restaurant. These things can be functional barriers, like conflating sex and gender in questions in a way that excludes transgender people, or more subtle messages that this service is not a safe place for your users by the use of exclusively white heterosexual images in marketing material. Either way, your user is either unable to or feels unsafe to use your service.

Implicit biases – caused by the all-too-often monoculturalism of our organisations – can often creep into the deepest depths of our services without us even knowing they're there. A great example of this came in 2015, when Google launched its long awaited Photos app. Google's developers had been working hard on an extra feature in the app that they were very proud of – an artificial intelligence (AI) algorithm that automatically tagged images with whatever was in them. Pictures of celebrating students were tagged as 'graduation', city scenes featuring skyscrapers as were tagged with 'skyscrapers' and any artfully composed photos of brunch were tagged 'food'. All hugely useful when you're searching for a picture.

It was only when Jacky Alciné, a Californian software developer, tested the feature on his own photos was it discovered that the tagging algorithm had a fatal flaw. Programmed by a predominantly white team, the AI identified Jacky, and all of his Black friends as 'gorillas'.

Jacky took to Twitter, and Google quickly removed the 'gorilla' tag, presumably realising that marginalising the world's people of colour might just outweigh the need to identify a rare primate. The tag was gone, but Google's photo AI remained racially biased, because its programmers were racially biased. They hadn't thought to test their product with people who weren't white – presumably nature-loving – men because that was what they were.

As a multinational organisation that supports the lives of billions of people around the world, to not test a product with a representative group of the world's population has disastrous effects, shifting an entire population's understanding of itself, and others.

Google isn't the first company to do this. Kodak famously altered the perceptions of an entire generation in the 1960s and 1970s by producing photographic film that couldn't take pictures of anyone with dark skin. Exclusion like this is caused by discrimination. Not the active kind that is a result of conscious hatred, but the subtler, more corrosive kind where we are so surrounded by a monoculture of people like ourselves that we fail to even notice that there are people with different needs to our own.

Inclusion is about more than just accessibility

This is why we need to go beyond thinking about accessibility, with all of the inherent biases that come along with creating a baseline of 'normal' versus those with 'access needs', and start to think in terms of 'inclusion' of a full spectrum of needs instead.

With services, it's also important to consider how all of these needs will affect each user across each channel, rather than just looking at the experience of a digital service.

Understanding how to make your service inclusive to people in all of these situations is both vital and complex to achieve.

If we relied only on people who look like us and have the same experiences as us to use our services, we'd be unlikely to have many users. But inclusion is hard and we all have a vastly diverse spectrum of differences from one another. How do you know what all of these are and – more importantly – how do you pick out a pathway to improve your service through all of this?

The first step is to recognise that there there are some user groups and characteristics that, because of their lack of representation in organisations, are more vulnerable to discrimination than others. This means that their needs are less likely to have been considered as part of a natural process of service improvement and need to be thought about more actively.

Nothing replaces the need to do research with your users to understand what specific barriers they might face when dealing with your service, however, there are some common types of barriers that may mean people find it more difficult to access your service. These things have to do with a number of different characteristics about a person: who they are – identity-defining characteristics, including age, gender, race and religion; what they can do – capabilities such as hearing, sight or reading ability; and things they have or have had access to – such as time, money, transportation or support from friends and family.

All of these things change the way we interact with services. A user who is deaf and has transportation, money and support from their family has very different needs to someone who is unemployed, lives alone and has dementia. Some of these characteristics are permanent or change very rarely – like someone's ethnic background or religion – and some change momentarily – like access to transportation or having a quiet space to make a phone call. Crucially, though, we will all experience some form of challenge at some point in our lives.

The following is a good place to start when identifying the reasons why someone might be more likely to be excluded from your service:

What they can do

Instead of particular 'conditions' or 'disabilities', which can often lead to generalisations, try to think about someone's strengths and weaknesses. Try to consider both short-term reasons why someone might have these issues and longer-term ones, as both groups are likely to have very different adaptation strategies to deal with their particular mix of abilities. These might be things like the ability to see, read, talk, hear, remember things, get somewhere physically or cope with loud spaces.

Who they are

These things change less often than the things you can do, but they still change. Make sure you allow users to see themselves represented and considered at every point of your service and allow them to adapt the way you see them when their life circumstances change.

Be careful about using these characteristics to define a different journey through a service for a particular user. Only do this where absolutely necessary. Make sure your user can change these characteristics at any point. Give people enough flexibility in your definitions or categorisations to see themselves represented.

These things will be things like someone's ethnic background, gender identity, sex, sexual orientation, age or religion.

What they have

These are the things that someone has at their disposal to use. They can be characteristics of their personality, or physical real-world assets that allow them to do something or not.

These are things like time, money, transportation, family and friends, but also self belief, civic literacy and education.

The second step to making sure your service is inclusive is to understand why it isn't already, and to tackle the underlying causes for this. Making sure everyone who needs to use your service can do so should seem like an obvious thing to do – so why is it so hard?

The truth is, when everything is going well with your service, it's easy to prioritise making sure it's inclusive. But when deadlines are short, there's not enough money or there are technical restrictions, things can unravel. In the context we now work in, this is sadly the norm.

In scenarios like this, phrases like 'you can't boil the ocean' or 'think about the 80/20 rule' start to creep into conversations and, before you know it, making the service inclusive of needs that are unlike that of the team designing the service have been deprioritised. The kind of implicit bias that drives these decisions

Inclusion is a necessity, not an enhancement

is why diversity within service teams is so important to meeting the diverse needs of the people who need to use our services.

Another reason why we often find it hard to justify making our services inclusive is because we see this as an enhancement for a small number of users, not a necessity for everyone. In reality, making your service inclusive doesn't just make it usable for diverse users, but for everyone.

The first reason for this is because the needs of users often converge. As we saw before, someone who isn't able to use the phone might find this difficult because they are autistic, deaf or at work while your call centre is open. Individually, each one of these groups represents a small number of users, and can sometimes be hard to justify meeting the needs of when timelines are tight, but together they represent a large portion of users.

This is true of more restrictions on your service than you might think, and to ignore them risks large portions of your users not able to use your service.

Secondly, testing your service with users with the most extreme 'edge-case' needs makes sure your service works for those in the most standard needs.

There is a strong history of doing this kind of testing in product design. Cars are driven into walls, credit cards are burned and sat on with massive bum-replicating machines, and the caps of chemical bottles are tested with children to make sure they can't be opened by someone who's unaware of their contents.

A perfect example of this is one very famous vegetable peeler that was developed by Betsey Farber, more than 25 years ago. In the summer of that year, Betsey was cooking with her husband Sam in a holiday cottage in France.

Betsey, who was apparently making an apple tart at the time, had had arthritis for a number of years and found using the peeler overly complicated and painful. Rather than suffer using a product that didn't work, she decided to experiment with improving the handle, adding pieces of clay until it was easier to grip.

Betsey's husband happened to be a (very recently) retired kitchenware entrepreneur who was bored of retirement and, after extensive research, hundreds of models and dozens of design iterations, one of the highest-selling kitchenware products was born.

The Oxo Good Grips Swivel Peeler has a thick rubbery handle that makes it better for everyone to use. It raised the bar for inclusive product design, and changed the way kitchen tools were designed. It gained such success that it was was inducted into MoMA's permanent collection in 1994 and, three decades after its release, still sells by the millions in many countries around the world. This kind of testing in extreme conditions makes our products safe and effective; the same is true of services.

Instead of thinking about designing for the 80% of needs that are easily met, we should spend our time with the 20% of needs that are these so-called outliers to understand how those in the most difficult circumstances can carve a pathway through our services that is easier for everyone to use.

Barriers to using your service come in many shapes and forms. Some will completely stop a user from using your service with immediate effect, while others might mean someone will endeavour to try and later struggle with an overwhelming feeling that they aren't welcome.

Sometimes, our services might be inclusive of someone's needs if they're using a very specific piece of technology, but when they switch to another channel or a mobile browser, they'll be unable to use your service.

It's important therefore not to think about inclusion as something your service is or isn't, but a scale that progressively means that your user can not only use your service, but feel safe, welcome and – importantly – use it in a way that makes them feel equal to all other users who might need to use that service.

It's equally important to remember that inclusion doesn't always mean making everyone do something in the same way. Sometimes, different users will need a different pathway through your service. Because it works better for them. The story of the invention of braille is a perfect reminder of this.

Braille was famously invented by Louis Braille whilst he was studying at the Royal Institution for Blind Youth in Paris. Having lost his sight in an accident as a child, Braille was incredibly inquisitive about ways that he could make the world around him – a pretty hostile place at the time – a better place for a person with no or limited sight. In 1821, Braille learned of a communication system devised by Captain Charles Barbier of the French Army to introduce a secret form of writing that allowed sailors to communicate at night without sight or sound, Braille immediately leaped upon the idea. He worked tirelessly until he'd perfected a language that was better than the one used by soldiers – reducing the military language from a 12-dot system to a 6-dot system, meaning that letters could be read with just one finger.

But for as long as blind people have been reading, the technology that has been used to enable this has been contentious, and it was another 30 years before the braille system was adopted in France, and another 50 years before it was in wide use in the US and the rest of Europe.

The reason was a man called Samuel Gridley Howe – a sighted man who ran a school for the blind in the US, who objected to the idea that there was a separate language for blind people that was unreadable to those who were sighted. Howe thought that braille would divide blind and sighted people, and that the system was overly complex. Instead, he invented a letter-based system called Boston Line Type – a printed alphabet with raised, embossed letters that could be read by sighted and non sighted people alike.

But Howe was guilty of 'talking to the fingers in the language of the eyes' and presuming that, as a sighted person, he knew what was best for blind and partially sighted people.

The crucial difference between Boston Line Type and braille (aside from the fact that braille was easier to read for non-sighted people) was that you could write in braille using a small inexpensive punch-tool. With Boston Line Type, you needed a huge expensive printer to emboss the letters, which meant that blind and partially sighted people could consume literature, but not contribute to it. Howe's students started passing letters to each other in braille (handily illegible to the sighted teacher) and used it to write their essays and homework. Eventually Howe admitted defeat. As it turned out, he didn't implicitly know what was best for people not like himself.

We can see Braille and Howe's competing systems as a lesson in understanding user needs (and not presuming you know best without first understanding someone's problems) but we can also see it as an example of how sometimes, making sure that everyone can use a service equally doesn't mean that they have to use it in the same way.

Making a service that is equal doesn't just happen instantly. There are several steps to making sure your service works in this way:

1 **Make sure your service is safe**
   Is the service a place where this user feels that their needs are understood and represented in a way that makes them feel as if they will be accepted and comfortable using your service?

2 **Make sure your service is perceivable**
   Can they physically access the information required to understand what they need to do? Is it available to one of their senses (sight, hearing or touch)?
   As an example, if the information is provided as text, someone that has sight needs to be able to see it. If someone has no sight, the text needs to be available in a format that means a screen reader can convert it to audio and an electronic braille device can convert it to touch.

3 **Make sure your service is understandable**
   Once the user is able to perceive the information and instructions available to them, can the user understand what they need to do by understanding the instructions they've been given?

4 **Make sure your service is operable**
   This is the benchmark of minimum service to your user – can they actually use it unaided?
   For example, if someone is using a keyboard, can they still do everything that someone using a mouse can do? Can someone who can't use the phone make changes to their account details in the same way as someone who can?

5 **Make sure your service is robust**
   Can the user use the service in any channel or technology they choose to use? For web pages, this might mean that the service works as expected in the technology that someone is using, regardless of what that technology is.

6   Make sure your service is equal

Does the service treat this person as if they were equal
to any other user? Or does it sideline them into another
service or experience that is less than the main service?

Lastly, inclusion isn't an afterthought to your service and can't
be thought about only when you're testing your service. It's both
easier and more effective to do at the beginning as some high-
level aspects to your service, which aren't changeable by visual
or interaction design, may affect your users.

Inclusion is like making blueberry muffins – it's a lot easier to put the blueberries in at the start than at the end.

Cordelia McGee-Tubb

Lack of diversity in your team

= lack of inclusion in your service

12

A good service encourages the right behaviours from users and staff

The service should encourage safe, productive behaviours from users and staff that are mutually beneficial. For users, the service should not set a precedent for behaviours that may put the user at harm in other circumstances – for example, providing data without knowing its use. For staff, this means they should not be incentivised to provide a bad service to users, for example, through short call-handling time targets.

As he prepared for his 2005 election campaign, then UK Prime Minister Tony Blair took to the stage in the BBC *Question Time* studio to go head to head with his Conservative Party opposition.

In the audience that night was Diana Church, who asked a question. She'd been trying to get a GP appointment for the past 3 weeks, unsuccessfully. Not because there weren't any appointments, but because her doctor had refused to book her an appointment in advance.

'You can't make the appointment in a week's time because you are only allowed to make it 48 hours beforehand,' she said. 'You have to sit on the phone for 3 hours in the morning trying to get an appointment because you are not allowed to ask for an appointment next week. All because they're trying to meet government targets.'

Blair responded that he was 'shocked', saying that this was 'probably an isolated incident'. He'd campaigned heavily on the improvements that the Labour Party had made to the NHS in its previous term in government, including a new target for GP surgeries to give all patients an appointment within 48 hours of calling their doctor. To settle the argument, the presenter asked the audience if they had experienced anything similar. Almost every hand went up.

Blair's response was priceless: 'Well, obviously it wasn't supposed to work like that.' In fact, there was no 'obviously' about it. The Labour Party had given GP surgeries a very clear target – make sure people can get an appointment in 48 hours.

To meet that target in the most effective way possible, surgery managers across the country had banned advance bookings to keep their appointments free for people calling 48 hours in advance.

The target was seen as a 'success' to Blair and his government, but this was because only those people who managed to sit through the hours of waiting to successfully get an appointment were recorded, while those who didn't – like Diana Church – weren't. The target was met, but the point was lost.

The 48-hour target was abolished five years later, and became a poster child for removing unhelpful government targets from the NHS. Its memory stands as a perfect example of how narrow targets and objectives, designed as proxies for the quality of your

What gets measured gets done

service, can easily motivate entirely the wrong type of behaviour. If you give people a target, they will inevitably try to meet that target, regardless of whether it helps to achieve the thing they're setting out to do.

This is true of some of the most fundamental targets in our organisations – from call-handling times for call centre workers that force operators to get rid of customers without fully answering their questions, to up-sale targets in shops that cause customers to take longer to pay at the till because they're bombarded with additional questions about offers. What we measure is invariably what gets done in our organisations.

In the case of the NHS, the problem wasn't that the outcome they wanted to achieve was wrong, but that it was communicated and recorded in a way that disincentivised the outcome that everyone in the NHS was trying to get to – that patients were able to see a doctor when they needed to.

These kinds of top-down targets are often implemented in such a way that – though the objective your organisation wants to get to might be well-known at the highest level – they're rarely communicated to the staff who need to deliver it. Instead, the upper levels of management will generally try to ensure that objectives are met by setting a target, forgetting entirely that those delivering the service might be the best at knowing how to measure whether they're being effective, so long as they understood the objective they're trying to meet.

Worse still, if these targets stay in place for any length of time, we can soon forget what the objective was in the first place, creating a kind of mirage on the horizon that's just to the left or right of what we're trying to achieve.

Whether you're trying to improve health and wellbeing of your users, or help to give them access to good, cheap ingredients to cook with, the most important thing is that you know what you're trying to achieve so you then understand what kind of behaviours you want to encourage. After all, there's no way that an objective can be encouraged without first knowing, and crucially remembering, what that thing is.

As we talked about at the beginning of this book, a good service is good for the user of the service (in that it does what they need it to do, in a way that works for them); good for the organisation providing it (in that it's profitable and easy to run); and good for society as a whole (in that it does not destroy the world we live in, or negatively affect the society as a whole).

The 'right' behaviours are ones that encourage each of these things. However, knowing what your objective is doesn't necessarily ensure that it happens, as Tony Blair found when he tried to make it easier to get an appointment with a GP.

You might set out with the best of intentions, but subtle things about the way your service works, is funded or the way you encourage your staff to do a good job, can all have an impact on whether you reach that goal, for you and your users.

What are the 'right' behaviours?

It's really important therefore, to know what we mean by 'right behaviours'.

What the 'right' behaviours are for your service will depend entirely on what you are trying to achieve. For example, 'right' in the context of a health service will mean behaviours that help a user to improve or maintain their current level of health. If you're a supermarket, right might mean helping your users to spend less time on groceries, and more time on other things.

Establishing 'right' for your service will of course be a subjective process, but to help you think about what this might mean, try to think about these as being behaviours that both encourage your service to be financially sustainable, and have a positive impact on the user and the world they live in. What's important to remember though is that these behaviours are inextricably linked. It's almost impossible to help your user do something in a way that doesn't have a negative impact on the world around them if your organisation isn't motivated to do the same. Likewise, it's almost impossible for your service to be financially sustainable if it is having a negative impact on the world around it. The behaviour of your users, your staff and your organisation as a whole are an ecosystem that is designed in a way that everyone in the system benefits from meeting your objective.

When building a service, there are four types of 'right behaviours' you need to think about encouraging:

Behaviours that benefit the user
Behaviours that help your user to achieve what it was they set out to achieve in a way that doesn't encourage them to take on behaviours that put them at immediate or future risk.

For example, for a diabetic patient using a healthcare service, this might mean creating a service that encourages them to take proactive steps to adapt their diet using a mobile monitoring service, but making sure that they are providing their data in a way that doesn't encourage them to accept sharing personal data with any company as the norm.

Behaviours that benefit your staff
Behaviours that that benefits the people who work for it. For example, if a person does a good job or takes initiative to change something proactively, they are rewarded.

Behaviours that help the company to be sustainable
Crucially, all of these things are impossible unless your organisation provides your service in a way that is sustainable. For commercial companies, this will mean that your service is profitable, and in a way that means you are not using up resources that cannot be used in the future. For charities or public organisations, it will mean that your service is sustainable within the amount of money you have (or are able to generate).

Behaviours that benefit the world, or at least do no harm
Your service doesn't encourage your user or your staff to do anything that is harmful to society or environment in which they live.

Gaining organisational alignment around all four of these areas is incredibly hard and we've made many attempts in the past at creating structures that enable this to happen more easily.

KPIs and targets have existed for millennia, but it wasn't until the 1990s that there was a formal documentation of linking individual performance with organisational performance. The 'balanced scorecard', created by Robert Kaplan and David Norton, was one of the first examples of this. Influenced by the work done by General Motors and other companies in the 1950s, the balanced scorecard was the first time individual targets were added up to an overall sense of company success and became the first 'modern' KPI framework.

In the late 1990s, hospitals in Pennsylvania and New York adopted this approach, hoping to enable patients to make better choices about which surgeon they should use. Unlike the UK and Europe, where you are likely to be assigned a surgeon by a hospital, your surgeon's previous history and successes are very important in the US where you're able to choose (depending on your insurance) which doctor you want to see. In order to give patients better clarity over who they should choose, hospitals decided to create an open 'report card' for the performance of individual doctors and the hospitals they worked in, allowing patients to see the success rates in surgery of the doctors they were choosing.

But in surgery, the success is not just to do with the skill of the surgeon (in fact, recent research has shown that this has the smallest effect of almost every other factor); it also reflects the health of the patient.

What hospitals found was that in order to increase their score, surgeons became more likely to operate on patients that were healthy, rather than those that were sick, which over time reduced the quality of care patients were likely to receive.

Targets can be a difficult way to encourage the right behaviours, even when they are seemingly in alignment from staff to your overall organisation. The missing link here was the user; understanding what needed to be done to ensure that they got the best possible care, then measuring that. This story shows how critical it is to not only make sure your behavioural incentives are in alignment, but that none are missed.

The New York and Pennsylvania hospitals focused purely on encouraging the right behaviours in users (choosing a good surgeon) but failed to think about how they might encourage the right behaviours of staff, their organisation or what effect this might have on the world at large. If they hadn't spotted the issue, might we have seen a world where patients who were more

A good service is good for everyone

Users

Staff

Your organisation

The world

sick were turned away from the best hospitals, and subsequently the lesser 'performing' hospitals would go on to receive fewer and fewer payments from the government and insurers?

More often than not, ensuring the organisation is working in a way that is sustainable, both financially and in terms of its resources and effect on the world is often missed when we think about 'behaviours'. A perfect example of this is our current understanding of who is ultimately responsible for our consumption of single-use plastics. It's now commonplace for consumers to feel that it they need to proactively avoid plastics – to use paper straws, avoid plastic coffee cups and to recycle at home – but the attitude that consumers are responsible for their own plastic consumption hasn't always been the case.

In 1953, the term 'litterbug' became common parlance for someone who drops litter, but its adoption into our collective psyche wasn't by accident. The term was popularised by a group called 'Keep America Beautiful', funded by some of the world's largest drinks manufacturers like Pepsi and Coca-Cola.

The organisation was founded in 1953, at the same time US states like Vermont were creating legislation to stop drinks from being sold in single-use plastic – thinking that was way ahead of its time in the 1950s. The group lobbied for consumer recycling (rather than reduced plastic use in packaging) for 20 years until finally, in 1971, they produced an advert that was so powerful, it would become one of the most watched adverts of all time.

The 'Crying Indian' advert featured a Native American (actually played by an Italian actor) who, while kayaking around a pristine forest (which happened to be next to a highway) gets hit by a bag of rubbish. The camera pans up to see the man crying and the narrator kicks in with the final message 'people start pollution, people can stop it'.

This environmental message was so effective that it spurred a generation of consumer guilt that hid the responsibilities of industry to adopt behaviours that would have improved the lives of individuals and society as a whole. It would take another 40 years for society to remember that the people who were responsible for this behaviour were not just consumers, but the corporations that serve them.

Regardless of your stance on corporate responsibility versus profiteering, it is no longer financially sustainable (if it ever was) to produce services that have a limited supply of materials, or will create a world that puts your users at risk. Not if you want them to survive long enough to pay for your service, at any rate.

It's all too common to force upon users a behaviour that should in fact be a behaviour that an organisation acts on itself. Users shouldn't have to fight against a negative behaviour of a company any more than a member of staff should have to fight to provide a good service for users, as we've seen in Pennsylvania hospitals and UK GP surgeries.

Some organisations have thankfully come to realise this, and have started to use targets focused on what a user is trying to achieve by using things like the 'jobs to be done' methodology by Anthony W Ulwick – which tasks organisations to organise their metrics around whether or not they are achieving an outcome for a user.

However, these outcome-focused targets very rarely change the overall structure of organisations and their alignment to doing good for users and the world in which they live. This is because targets form just one of the many ways in which user, staff and organisational behaviour can be encouraged to work together towards a better outcome. There are three main ways we can have an influence on user, staff and organisational behaviour:

Incentives and KPIs

As we've seen in this section, targets and financial incentives can have a huge effect on the way in which staff behave and the service we provide to users. We often have the impression that knowing something gives us control of it, and as we've seen this is far from the case.

Things that can have a negative effect on your user:
- Incentivising your staff to work in a way that runs counter to delivering benefits for your user.

Business model

How organisations are financially motivated has a huge effect on who that organisation treats as its customer and therefore what sort of service they provide to those people. At a business that is paid for by investors, those investors are the customer; for a business that makes money through advertising, the advertisers, too, are the customer.

Things that can have a negative effect on your user:
- Business models that encourage consumption of unreplaceable resources.
- Business models that are funded by people other than your customer directly.

Interactions and heuristics

The structure of your service, or the way you interact with a service, can have a huge effect on your user and on their ability to achieve the outcome they need to in a way that doesn't have a detrimental effect on others.

Things that can have a negative effect on your user:
- Getting your user to do things that would be dangerous to do with another organisation they don't trust, or teaching dangerous practices to your users that put them in harm.
- Things like getting them to sign over their data or accept internet tracking without consent.
- Incentivising your user to work in a way that is harmful to your sustainability or to the world around them.

It's common for organisations to see changing user behaviour alone as a tool to achieving a better outcome. We've seen the potentially harmful effects this can have when a company attempts to do this in a way that means they don't need to change themselves with 'Keep America Beautiful'.

Sometimes our services are designed in such a way that they either encourage or discourage a user from doing something without the user knowing what's happened. These 'dark patterns', a term coined by the user research specialist Harry Brignull, can

be seen everywhere from airline websites that force you to opt out of buying travel insurance or newsletters that bury a tiny 'unsubscribe' button deep within their small print.

It's no mistake that Amazon, which patented the one-click purchase back in 1999, requires would-be escapees from the service to click on a minimum of eight unmarked links at the bottom of the page before they can delete their Amazon account. These things rely on a principle of the 'path of least resistance' or 'choice architecture' as Richard Thaler and Cass Sunstein write in their 2008 book 'Nudge'. A principle so influential to business and governments alike that in 2010 then UK Prime Minister David Cameron set up the 'nudge unit' (or Behavioural Insights Team) within Number 10 to improve outcomes for users and reduce spending for government.

The team has had huge successes, such as the dramatic increase in the number of organ donations, when users are asked to opt out rather than opt in to organ donation as part of getting their driving licence.

But behavioural manipulation can have a darker side. Nudge principles have been used to create what has been coined 'the hostile environment' for immigrants to the UK – nudging people away from interacting with the welfare state and creating a sprawling bureaucracy to deter immigrants from living in Britain. Regardless of your opinions on immigration, dark patterns often allow organisations to say one thing, while doing something completely different.

Although nudging a user's behaviour is often done with the best intentions, both dark patterns and 'nudge' share a common principle – that it is OK to manipulate your user's behaviour without their knowledge, for the 'greater good'. Regardless of whether this greater good is making money or improving organ donation, it's a slippery slope to start believing it's OK to manipulate people without their consent, so long as your intentions are sound.

So if manipulation of user behaviour isn't the answer to creating better outcomes for users, society and your organisation, and neither are narrowly defined targets or misaligned business models, what is the answer?

The answer is honesty.

Building a service that encourages users, staff and organisations to act responsibly – while being clear about your service's intentions.
To do this though, we need to understand each element of 'encouragement' at our disposal, from KPIs to financial models and design decisions. Most crucially of all though, we need to understand that these need to be in alignment with one another to work.

When thinking about encouraging the right behaviours in users and staff in order to achieve the outcome you've set out to achieve:

1   Remember what you're trying to achieve.

2   Make sure you focus on balancing the behaviours you expect of your users with the behaviours you expect of your staff and your organisation. Don't just focus on one of these.

3   Make sure that the outcome you want to achieve is encoded in every layer of your organisation, from its business model and staff targets, right down to the way your users interact with your service.

13

A good service should respond to change quickly

The service should respond quickly and adaptively to a change in a user's circumstance and make this change consistently throughout the service. For example, if a user changes their phone number online, their new phone number should be recognised in a face-to-face service.

It's not often that a chief operating officer (COO) loses their job when a service fails. Far more likely it will be the chief executive officer (CEO), or almost any other executive that gets the chop when things go wrong. COOs are the type of person you might blame for bad accounting software, but not a whole company failure.

But this wasn't the case for Michael Hickey when he was forced to resign after a 30-year career with Ryanair. Hickey was responsible for a 'computer malfunction' – as it was reported in the press – of a piece of holiday booking software that left nearly 80,000 people stranded in airports in June 2018.

The problem started months earlier when Hickey had overseen a change to Ryanair's staff management tool. The tool had one small but crucial flaw. It didn't recognise or alert managers to patterns in staff holiday bookings.

This meant that, at the busiest point of the year for Ryanair, when most people in the northern hemisphere take a summer holiday, it had no idea that most of its cabin crew were also on holiday. There simply weren't enough people to fly and crew their aircraft. Ryanair tried recalling staff where it could, but passengers were still stranded for another 24 hours while they waited for their pilot and crew to come back to work.

As a travel operator, you would have thought that the idea that most people want to take their holidays in the summer months wouldn't come as a surprise. However, this is precisely what Ryanair's holiday booking tool did not account for.

Our lives are chaotic and constantly changing. We need to take holidays, get married, divorced, change our names, genders, phone numbers and addresses. Some of these these changes become predictable when we look at them on a massive scale – such as the likelihood we'll take a holiday between June and September. Once we know these things will happen, we can design for them in our service – like in the case of Ryanair, having some kind of time management tool for managers to see who's on holiday when.

But just as there are changes in our lives that are predictable and easy to design around, there are also changes that aren't, because there simply isn't a pattern for when they'll happen at a larger scale. These things can be big significant changes, like changes to your name or gender, or they can be smaller and more incidental to our lives, like a change to your our credit card or phone number. These changes aren't necessarily predictable, but they do happen. And, because we know they happen, we can expect them and make sure that our services respond to them when they do.

The most common problem with these less predictable changes is that we don't expect them to happen at all.

At-home health check company Thriva is a perfect example of how difficult this can be when not managed properly.

We've seen how Thriva (which tests users' general health and wellbeing in the comfort of their own home) manages its use of county pathology labs well to provide an integrated, silo-less service in principle 7. However, few services are perfect and Thriva has struggled with one particular aspect of their service – keeping up with changes in its users' lives.

Thriva offers a variety of different tests – from nutritional checks to diabetes and cholesterol levels. However, by asking for their user's biological sex, Thriva presumes its customers' gender. This wasn't necessarily a problem until in late 2018 it announced its new hormone checking service by sending marketing materials for fertility tests and hormone balances to trans men, and women who had identified as 'female'. One such test that checked for 'female sex drive' even came complete with aubergine emojis.

A change in a user's life, combined with a change in its service suddenly saw what was a well-constructed and empathetic user experience become one that caused dysphoria to many.

Thriva (at the time of writing) offers no way for its users to change their gender, or indeed provide a different sex to their gender, meaning that this is a change Thriva simply didn't consider would happen.

In the case of both Ryanair and Thriva, both of the changes they responded to were key pieces of information that were needed to make a decision within a service – in these cases, is this person suitable for gender-based hormone tests, or a holiday?

While not all changes in a user's life will affect how they use your service, not all changes in your users' lives will be something that you need to know to make a decision about them. It's important to consider both types of change when designing a service.

When designing for changes in a user's life, it's useful to think about two major types of changes:

Changes that affect your service directly

For example, if your service is helping users to book holidays at work. Something that affects your service is your user's ability to take a holiday at a certain time. Changes like this affect the direct outcome of your service and so affect the functionality of your service and how it works.

Think carefully about what pieces of information you use to anchor the identity of your user within your service – their name, gender, age, location, address and phone number can all change. Your service should respond to changes to these areas as much as it does to indirect changes.

Changes that affect your service indirectly

There are also a number of things that will change in your user's life that have an indirect effect on your service. Continuing with the example of a device that helps you book holidays – if your user goes through a divorce and decides to take time off to recover, this might not affect the fact that they are booking annual leave, but might affect how your service speaks to them about it.

These things won't change the functionality of your service, but will change how that functionality works. For example, rather than a confirmation email sent to them under their previous name, your service might need to opt for more neutral language and enable users to change their name when booking.

It's important to consider both of these scenarios when thinking about how your service deals with change. In both cases, planning for these things to change is vital. Facebook's complex web of sharing permissions and access settings is a good example of what can happen when something changes in someone's life in a way that, although it might not affect your service directly, hasn't been planned for at all. In particular, the story of Alysha Soames, a freshman student from Milwaukee, Wisconsin in the US.

When Alysha moved to Madison to go to college, her life underwent massive changes. Like most teenagers moving away from home for the first time, she tried new things and developed

How you check
if something
has changed
is as important
as making sure
your service
responds to that
change

her interests in ways that she hadn't thought of before. One of these things was the realisation that she was gay. Making friends is hard in college, especially when you're new to a group, so Alysha joined an LGBTQ+ choir to try and meet other people.

Her family was following her progress at college on Facebook, but were deeply conservative. When she was invited to be friends with her choir on Facebook by the choirmaster one evening, she had no idea that her family could see the invite and, in one instant, her new identity was revealed.

For many LGBTQ+ people who are from families or cultures where they're not accepted, this information is potentially life threatening. For Alysha, it meant her family disowned her. This story could have had a far more tragically than it did. Thankfully Alysha went on to lead a happy life in Austin, Texas. But what it highlights is that it's not just the information we use actively in our services to make decisions – like how we're identified, contacted or referred to – we need to think about what happens when things change.

Any change in a user's life can have an effect on the way they interact with your service – whether that's their sexuality, gender, location or income – and needs to be thought of when you consider the functional elements of your service, like how users share information about themselves. These changes may not be predictable, but we can expect them and build them into the fabric of the way our service works.

Changes that affect your service directly and indirectly need to be considered in the way your service is designed to make sure that your service doesn't accidentally cause harm to your user, or stop them from using your service.

What we've seen with Facebook is that sometimes not everything needs to change consistently everywhere; sometimes we want multiple identities.

When changes happen in our lives, we face a decision – who to tell, and who not to tell. These are incredibly personal decisions but are crucially based on why someone needs to know, and what they will do with that information. All of this means it's important to know why that information is being asked for and what it will be used for.

Traditional early internet thinking led us to think that the best way of doing this was to create a customer account, where your user's details could be changed all in one place. However, this is certainly not the right way of dealing with indirect changes – you shouldn't have to tell Facebook, your bank or your supermarket that you're gay, but neither should you be treated by those organisations in a way that presumes you are not.

The prospect of telling an organisation something like this when there's no clear need for it is unnerving for obvious reasons, but the reality is – when anything changes in your user's life, no matter how small and insignificant, they are unlikely to tell your service unless there is a very clear benefit for them doing so – for example, updating their address so that they can still receive deliveries.

The UK government's DVLA knows this phenomena well, as nearly 1.3 million speeding fines are unpaid in the UK every year. While some speeding drivers avoid the penalty fine through other means – like opting to do a speed awareness course – most fines are left unpaid because they go to the wrong address.

In the UK, we move on average every 8 years. If you're renting, that number can be as much as once per year in some areas of the country. Add in the fact that the legal driving age in the UK is 17 and for the first few years of adult life after leaving home, many young people opt to keep their main address as their parents' address, and you have a recipe for misdirected fines.

The DVLA has a service that allows you to change your address but, other than receiving a new driving licence, there's very little reason to tell DVLA when you move house. In the UK you need to renew your licence every 10 years, meaning that most users will have moved at least once in that time.

DVLA's traditional approach to solving this has been to create an account that can be updated when your 'details' change. This is very much an early internet response to this, and in direct contrast to the way that many more recently changed services deal with this type of change.

In light of incidents such as what happened to Alysha, Facebook has since opted for a model that makes it clear what will happen to information at the point a user intends to share it.

This allows the user to have control over how the change in their life affects their relationship with the service at that moment in time, when this decision is relevant. It doesn't focus on what the change is – asking users to tell them if anything has changed – but on the effect it might have on someone's life, in this case, their ability to share information openly with everyone they know on Facebook, or a smaller group.

This method of changing your status with a service at the point that information is relevant, rather than at the point when that information changes, has also been adopted in one of the most high-stress 'appointment booking services' in the world – the UK's NHS.

Missed appointments cost the NHS £216m per year – the cost of two fully operational hospitals. To combat this it has introduced a policy of asking a patient if their phone number and address are the same before making any new appointment, rather than writing to users to update their address when it changes.

For changes to our service to work for both us and our users, they need to be dealt with not just quickly but at a point in time when the benefit of sharing this information is clear.

Crucially, for changes within our users' lives that indirectly affect our service, we need to understand and design for the effects these changes might have, without relying on our users to tell us anything.

Getting this balance right can be hard, so when thinking about how to manage both direct and indirect changes to your service it's useful to consider the following:

1   Some changes should be predicted, and some can be expected. Work on the assumption that nothing is fixed – make it easy for users to change things about themselves.
2   Make a list of all the changes that might happen to a user when using your service and work out which ones need to be directly designed for as functionality, and which don't. For those that don't, think about how they will affect the other aspects of your service.
3   For changes that directly change the way your service works, always give users the option of doing this at the point that this information becomes relevant, but always make sure they're aware of who knows about this change and what that information will be used for.
4   Not all change should be universal; always give users the ability to share only what they want to share with the people they want to share it with.

14

A good service clearly explains why a decision has been made

When a decision is made within a service, it should be obvious to a user why this decision has been made and clearly communicated at the point at which it's made. A user should also be given a route to contest this if they need to.

Carol Beer is sitting behind her desk at a travel agency, staring into the middle distance. A man walks in and asks if he can buy a flight to Alicante. Carol looks at him for a second, as if to dare him to ask again, then types furiously into her computer. Satisfied that the result is the one she always gets, she turns to face him. 'Computer says no,' she says, with a satisfaction that never seems to waver. The man looks at her, confused and, after weighing the options of trying to reason with her and escaping her glare, leaves the shop.

When David Walliams brought Carol Beer to life for British TV viewers in the show *Little Britain*, he was telling a story we have almost all experienced at one time in our lives. You're trying to do something, you're rejected by 'the system' and, after resorting to a human for support, you're given the ultimate conversation ender – 'I'm sorry that's just the way it is. There's nothing I can do.'

Carol represents the worst of our relationships with large, unyielding corporations and their seemingly 'jobsworth' front-line workers. She has become synonymous with everything we hate about them, but it's not her fault. Carol is one of millions of workers who are forced to be the mute avatars of machines that regularly make seemingly irrational decisions and rarely ever explain their actions. What else can Carol do – if the computer says no, it says no. She, and every other Carol, are the product of optimistic digitisation – our unwavering belief that machines can 'now as never before!' replace complex human decision-making.

The reason why Carol became such an institution of British comedy was that her story was so familiar. But, in reality, the interaction between decision-making – whether computer-based or not – and our needs in the real world aren't so funny.

The decisions made by services are often based on a complex number of inputs. Even in simple service interactions, such as whether or not you can use an airport lounge – can involve several factors including membership status or number of air miles. In a bid to standardise decisions across multiple services, we often create policies, processes or even scripts to make sure our decisions about different users are consistent, no matter who is making those decisions.

Today, these decisions – often codified as algorithms – are based on an unprecedented amount of information about us; not just about what's in our shopping baskets, but who we are and what we like, how we speak to each other and our deepest fears. Not only do these algorithms have an unprecedented amount of information though, they also have an unprecedented amount of control to make decisions in the most important aspects of our daily lives – from banking to healthcare. This new, invisible decision-making infrastructure is starting to pose questions that reveal weaknesses in the way we make and communicate decisions in our services.

A good example of this is our modern judicial system, where algorithms have been used to assist the decision-making process since the 1930s. Computerised decision-making dates back a long way for good reason – the entire court system is geared around predictions – particularly when it comes to sentencing, which is largely based on your likelihood to commit another crime in the future. Likewise, many of our modern judicial systems around the world are designed to remove as much human bias as possible – from having a jury of our peers judge us, to the inability to refer back to previous convictions in cases that aren't related.

But our increasing reliance on automated decisions – and crucially our lack of understanding of how they work – has led to huge weaknesses in the way we rely on these impartial decisions.

In 2017, investigative journalists at Propublica tested a set of US court sentencing algorithms and discovered that, despite the promised neutrality of decision-making compared to a human, the algorithm used by courts across the US gave much harder sentences to people of colour because, according to the data, they're more likely to commit another crime.

The fact that this is a self-fulfilling prophecy – where people of colour in the US are far more likely to be arrested and convicted by an already biased legal system – wasn't something that had been designed for. The algorithm was only as good as the information it was working on and, as we saw in principle 11, this is a classic example of what happens when you don't consider inclusion and diversity in the way you design. You would hope in that kind of situation a judge would see the flaws of the algorithm and know to overrule it, but spotting a problem that happens in micro integers over time is incredibly hard and is the reason why we're not seeing people standing up and trusting their own instincts over these automated rulings.

This effect was well-documented in the case of Christopher Drew Brooks, a 19-year-old man in the US who was convicted of the statutory rape of a 14-year-old girl. Christopher had apparently been in a consensual relationship with the girl at the time, according to both her own and witness testimony, but she was nonetheless underage, so he was convicted of a crime.

During his trial an algorithm assessed Christopher's likelihood of reoffending. Since he was only 19, and was already committing sexual offences, it concluded that there was a high chance he was going to return to a life of crime and recommended he be sentenced to 18 months in jail.

This particular algorithm placed a lot of weight on age. But if Christopher Drew Brooks had been 36, rather than 19, making him 22 years older than his victim – by most human logic making the crime much worse – the algorithm would have considered him a low risk of reoffending, thus giving him a much shorter sentence. However, when given a sentence much higher than average for the crime he had committed, no one challenged it, for the same reason that no one questions why people of colour are given much harder sentences by the same algorithmic decision-makers on a daily basis.

Individually, these biases are almost identical to the mistakes a human decision-maker might make, making them hard to spot. It's only over time that we start to notice a pattern. And yet, the law, like many of our other interactions with the world, is based on precedent. Meaning that if someone is sentenced in one way once, other people like them will probably continue to be until someone takes a new approach and sets a new precedent. In this world, if left unchecked, bad decisions replicate themselves.

As US Attorney General Eric Holder said in 2014, '[Automated decisions] may exacerbate unwarranted and unjust disparities that are already far too common in our criminal justice system and in our society.'

But what if it didn't take hundreds of people to go to jail for us to realise that a mistake had been made? If their logic was exposed, these flaws in decision-making would not only be a lot easier to identify, allowing staff in the court system to better override bad decisions, but the algorithms themselves would be able to be adapted and improved too.

The fact that decision-making isn't explained means that bad decisions can continue unchecked and unchanged. The harm doesn't happen when an algorithm is given too much power, but when its power isn't explained. This problem isn't just isolated to machine decisions by any means.

It's hard now to find a service that doesn't have rules and policies that sit behind it, no matter how open those are to interpretation. The decisions we make that are based on 'policy' are often equally as unexplained to both users and staff, allowing mistakes to be made unchecked.

The character Daniel Blake in Ken Loach's awardwinning film *I, Daniel Blake* is a perfect example of how this works within the British welfare system. The film is based on years of research of welfare system users. In it, Daniel's character, a 59-year-old carpenter from Newcastle, suffers a heart attack and is told not to go back to work by his doctor. To keep financially afloat, he tries to get access to disability payments. He doesn't qualify – in part because he misunderstands the meaning behind the health questions he has to answer and answers them in a way that, though truthful, isn't representative of his ability to work because of poorly worded questions.

Having been turned down for disability benefits, Daniel is then told he has to apply for Jobseeker's Allowance while he looks for work, unless he appeals the decision of the 'decision-maker'. What unfolds is a sorry story that ultimately leads to Daniel's death, as he waits for an appeal to the decision that – although it deems him unfit to work – comes moments too late.

Daniel's story represents the experience of millions of British people who have been deemed fit for work because they didn't understand that, when they were being asked 'can you walk the length of a shopping aisle?' or 'can you reach as high as the pocket in a shirt?', what they were actually being asked was 'are you able to work?'

Sadly this lack of transparency is by design, not by accident. In some cases, we actively believe if we explain our workings behind the questions we ask, and therefore the decisions we make, then

How you make a decision is as important as what decision you make

users will somehow use this knowledge to their advantage and start trying to game our rules. This is almost never true. It's almost always another cleverer bit of code that will outsmart your service, not a human being.

The character of Daniel Blake, not unlike many others interacting with the British social welfare system, couldn't give an honest answer to the questions he was asked, because the question hadn't been asked honestly in the first place. This meant that he couldn't be given an honest clear answer on why – despite being medically unfit for work – he was told that he must.

His future was in the hands of a faceless, nameless 'decision-maker', leaving him powerless in a system that is supposedly designed to create agency and self confidence to return to work. Crucially this left Daniel, and others like him, with no understanding of how he might take control of the situation, appeal it if it was wrong or improve his situation himself.

What Daniel Blake, Christopher Drew Brooks and the countless people of colour that have been heavily sentenced by algorithms in the US justice system tell us is that if you can't explain why you came to a decision, it's almost impossible for staff to change that decision, or for users to appeal it. Given how many of these decisions are wrong, this is a huge problem in the way we design our services.

We design our services in a way that demands 100% accuracy, and that just isn't realistic. People and machines make mistakes. But there's an even darker side to this interaction between unknown decisions and our expectations that causes even bigger problems.

In 1997 the AI team at IBM was gearing up for what was one of the most exciting moments in modern computing: a chess match.

This wasn't just any chess match. This was a match to settle a score, between the reigning world champion Garry Kasparov and the world's most powerful supercomputer – Deep Blue.

Kasparov and Deep Blue had played against each other a year earlier and Deep Blue had lost. The team had spent the last 3 years making improvements to Deep Blue and they wanted to prove a point – that if the odds were equally staked, a supercomputer could outsmart a super-chess player.

Kasparov was described by his peers as a god of chess, as much for his abilities, but for his presence in the room.

The match opened well, with Kasparov making some early gains. But as the match progressed, it became obvious that Kasparov was struggling. Then, in the second match, Deep Blue made a move that made no logical sense to Kasparov. He was visibly perturbed – sighing and rubbing his face – before he abruptly stood and walked away, forfeiting the match.

The reason Kasparov was beaten by the machine wasn't that the machine was better than him at chess. Chess experts almost universally agree that Kasparov was the better player – but the problem was, that Kasparov allowed himself to be intimated by the machine. Deep Blue had made a move that had no immediate gain. To Kasparov, this looked exactly like the kind of human intelligence that would plan strategic, short-term losses in order to win an overall match.

He later said he was riled by a move the computer made that was so surprising, so un-machine-like, that he was sure the IBM team had cheated. In short, Kasparov thought that Deep Blue was a lot smarter than it actually was.

Kasparov made a decision that cost him a match and, in part, his career, based on a decision that wasn't explained. A strategy that the IBM team designed to deliberately unnerve Kasparov and make it look as if Deep Blue had human-like intelligence. So human-like in fact that Kasparov forfeited the match because he assumed IBM was cheating.

Kasparov reacted the same way most of us would react when we're faced with a decision that isn't explained – we assume that the odds are stacked against us and that system is cheating.

There will always be a time when your service will need to make a decision about a user that will mean that they don't get what they'd hoped for. They've been turned down for a mortgage, or they're going to need to go through another unforeseen hurdle to reach their goal. Whatever it is, it is a decision that's been made about that user and their future. However small that decision might seem to you, it has the potential to change how much your user trusts you. It's how that decision is made, not that decision itself, which leads your user to either trust or not trust you.

Transparency of decision-making shows how a decision will affect a user in advance, and gives them the ability to take control of their situation, change their circumstances, go elsewhere or challenge your decision. For staff too, transparency means that they can override and challenge a decision, but only if they know how it works.

There are four things to watch out for when designing decision-making in your service:

1   Make sure your decisions are valid
    Always check your decisions for potential conflicts or dead ends. And for biases that are based on the information that is collected or used for decision-making.

2   Make sure your decisions are transparent
    Make it very clear to both users and staff what information has been used to make a decision and why this information is relevant for the types of decisions you need to make. It's a lot clearer what the task at hand is if you know why a question is being asked.
    Making your decisions transparent also means making sure that any staff who need to explain this to users later will be able to understand why this decision has been made.
    Some decisions are incredibly complex – like insurance premiums – so think about how to communicate these carefully. You can't expect your staff or your users to understand the finer points of risk measurement, but you can explain enough information to help them understand why a decision has been made.

3   Make sure your decisions are communicated
    Make sure that every decision you make about a user is clearly communicated to your user at the time it is made.
    All too often, users become aware that a past decision has been made about them that affects them now or in the future.

If you can, make sure every decision that is about to be made is clearly explained up front, giving your user a chance to course correct and change their circumstances if needed.

4   Make sure there's a way to appeal your decisions

Your decision-making process, whether algorithm-based or human won't always be right, neither will it be able to deal with extreme circumstances that need human judgement.

Make sure your user knows your staff have the ability to appeal a decision that they think is wrong. Even if there is little room for changing the final outcome, very little can replace the ability a human brain has to be able to make complex judgements.

For more info on why this is important, see principle 15.

Intimacy with machines requires trust; trust that they think in the same way as we do

15

A good service makes it easy to get human assistance

A service should always provide an easy route for users to speak to a human if they need to.

When Gina Haynes moved from Philadelphia to Texas with her boyfriend in 2010, she was excited about all of the changes the move would bring – a new house, new friends and a new job.

It was only when she applied to seven different jobs as an apartment manager that she realised that there was a problem. After successful interviews, she was turned down for every single one. Finally she called one of the prospective employers, who said she had failed a background check.

Confused, Gina started to investigate and found that she had been added to not just one, but several criminal record-checking services as having committed fraud.

A year earlier, she had bought a used Saab, and the day she drove it off the forecourt, smoke started pouring from the engine. The dealer charged $291 for repairs. When she refused to pay, the dealer filed fraud charges. Not wanting to face the even bigger legal fees to fight the case, Gina paid the fine.

Her record was clean, but unbeknownst to Gina, her court hearing was still listed on the county court's website. That website, and the information on it, had been used by several employment background ID checking agencies. The court's website was updated a week later, but Gina had no idea how many companies had downloaded the outdated data.

She spent hours calling background checking companies to see whether she was in their databases, but getting the information removed and corrected from so many databases was a daunting mission. Even if the record was corrected in one database, it would be wrong in another, unknown to Gina until a prospective employer requested information from it. But by then, the damage was done.

Gina has since found work as a customer service manager, but she says that's only because her latest employer didn't run a background check. She still phones every new background ID checking company she sees, just in case they have a copy of the old data from the county court's website.

The ultimate solution to Gina's problem would have been for the court to have tighter controls around who was able to use their data but, given that this didn't happen, the bare minimum service provided to Gina should have been for the court to have helped trace who might be using this information. However, after hours of searching for the right number to call, Gina couldn't get through to anyone who would assist. It either wasn't their problem, or they didn't know how to fix it.

Nine years later, in Burnley, UK, Laura Park had lost her husband Robert. Since he had died of cancer 6 months earlier, Laura decided the time was right to transfer all of his accounts into her name. Starting with the TV and broadband subscription.

Having managed to assign herself as the main account holder, she set down her chores for another day. The next morning, she woke up to an email in her inbox with the subject: 'It's never been a more exciting time to take over your Virgin Media account', which went on to describe all of the new TV shows that the cable television and broadband company was showing that month. Not only this, but her account name, which she thought would have changed, hadn't – rather than 'Laura' it was still 'Laura&Rob'.

Laura was devastated. Not knowing what to do, she phoned Virgin Media for help. Although still upset by the experience, she was redirected to Virgin Media's bereavement team, where they were eventually able to bypass the usual account permissions and make the changes she needed to her account.

Laura and Gina were both the victims of bad service design.

Gina's data was used without her consent, or the consent of the guardian of that data. She was then left without support or communication from the one organisation that should have helped.

Laura, on the other hand, was subjected to a service that didn't respond to her circumstances, and didn't factor in that the reason someone might move their account might be because the original account holder had died.

Although the reasons for their situation are different – what unites both of these stories is how they either were or weren't able to resolve their problems.

Laura was able to call Virgin Media, and although she was treated appallingly until she got there, she was eventually directed to a bereavement team who were able to bypass the usual procedure and help her change her account name and contact details. In contrast, Gina is still left in a no man's land with nowhere to turn except the next ID checking company that might have the wrong details for her. There was no one at the court who was able to take accountability for the failure or resolve the issue.

Every service fails at some point. Whether it's a temporary technical issue, poor design or an erroneous decision – if the path ahead isn't clear or easy to complete, your user will need some sort of help through it.

What differentiates your service is not whether or not it fails, but how it deals with failure when it happens

Getting access to an empowered person who can make a decision, and clearly explain that decision to you, is a vital part of this recovery.

Compared to humans, computers are perceived to follow rules and be unable to make judgement calls – particularly in complex situations that might sit outside of a standard procedure. In situations that users themselves define as 'complex', or a grey area that they don't know fits into your service, their preferences will always be to speak to a human decision-maker.

It's this capacity for complex reasoning, and even empathy when users face a confusing or complex task, that means they turn to human support – no matter how smart our automated decision-making. This is particularly relevant in a situation like Gina's – where the unfairness of her original story may well have provided some mitigating circumstances that the court may have responded to.

In essence, what we expect to get from a human is not what we expect to get from a machine.

Gone are the days when speaking to a human was our first point of call for accessing simple services. Google is the homepage to most services, whether they are based online or not.

This triage through digital channels, where it's often easier to answer quick questions, or complete a service unaided if we can, has changed what users need from human assistance. We are now far more likely to seek human assistance for problems or more complex issues than we are for general enquiries. The contradiction to this rule, however, is when our services are badly designed or inaccessible. In this instance we see far higher numbers of contacts based around general enquiries.

In a study conducted by the Government Digital Service in 2014, roughly 80% of the cost of government was spent on services. Not surprising, since government is the oldest and largest service provider in the UK. What was more surprising was that up to 60% of that cost was spent on calls and casework. Diving deeper still into these numbers, roughly 43% of these calls were status-chasing calls, 52% were questions about how to do something, 5% were complaints, but the smallest number by far were calls to do with complex cases, at just around 2% of total calls.

In essence, most human contact to our services is unnecessary, but generated by badly designed services that mean more people are entering the system than necesssary (generating delays to the service and subsequent status-checking calls) or are confused about what they need to do to achieve a certain outcome – the vast majority of which could be solved with clearer service design.

Hiding your phone number just pisses people off

Our solution to this has often sadly been to make it harder for users to contact us, rather than improving our services so that they don't need to – meaning that those who do need to contact us are faced with endless interactive voice response (IVR) scripts telling them to visit a website (when they often already have) or phone numbers that are hidden from the website entirely.

Of the top 10 banks in the UK, only 6 have a clearly visible phone numbers on their website. Retail is even worse, with only 4 out of 10 supermarkets and 2 out of 10 high-street clothing companies. But it isn't just our older pre-internet organisations that are creating ever-more difficult routes to speak directly to a human. Neither Amazon nor Ebay have a phone number you can call directly.

This has led to the creation of an entirely new service – internet phone number finders. The only problem is, these websites generally charge users an additional fee for their services to connect your user to you.

But this traditional route of accessing human or human-like assistance isn't the only area that's growing because of a lack of human assistance elsewhere.

Interacting with services in a conversational way has been recognised as a more efficient way of getting support to use a service, to the extent that we are now putting investment into human-like assistance.

The proliferation of chatbot services and in-home voice assistants that help us to interact with our banks, utilities and supermarkets has proliferated at an astounding rate over the past 10 years.

However helpful this method of interacting with a service is to users, what these methods don't replace is the ability to make a conscious, informed decision about something – whether that's to bypass the normal account rules because you've suffered a bereavement, where you should go next in your career or getting support with an addiction.

There is a diminishing value of automation for these types of scenarios, such that even if we develop the technology to do so, it's economically not feasible (or effective for users) to completely replace humans for the myriad increasingly complex input we need from real humans.

How much of your service needs to be human-based will depend on a few factors. Some services will be almost entirely human – addiction counselling, for example – and others almost not at all – like online clothes shopping.

There is no hard and fast rule for how much of your service needs to comprise of human versus machine-based interaction, but there are a number of factors that will increase the need for human contact within a service:

Services that are complex
No service should be overly complex, but some involve multiple decision points, options to weigh up or comparisons to make. The more complex your service, the more human assistance your users will need.

Services that are high risk
Situations of high risk often mean uncertainty for users and an increased need for being guided through a decision that may have a huge impact on their lives. Combining complexity and risk is a huge factor in the level of support needed.

Services that are high value
If your service is expensive, or carries some large financial risk – say benefit payments or wealth management – it is likely to have a dramatic impact on your users. Services in this category need support from trained staff who are able to advise on the best route forward.

Services that are tied to the physical world
If your service requires physical checks or needs your user to be present somehow – for example, at a hotel or a GP surgery,

Use computers and humans for what they're good at

your service will need more human contact. Digitally navigating the unpredictability of the physical world is hard to do alone.

It's important to get the balance right of human to digital in your service. Getting the balance wrong can happen in both directions.

The more humans that are involved in providing your service, the more expensive it becomes to scale, meaning that too much human contact and not enough automation can artificially incentivise your organisation to focus on users who exhibit only the most extreme cases.

This can occasionally mean only treating those with the biggest problems, or those with the most money. This may be suitable for your service if you're running a wealth management firm, or a drug treatment clinic specialising in chronic addiction, but perhaps not so suitable if your objective is to cater for a wider selection of society. Or scaling your impact to a large number of people under your current business plan, as we saw in principle 11, and making sure everyone can use your service.

Too little human decision-making or contact, however, can mean you end up accidentally focusing on users who have the simplest or most straightforward cases, or who can make their way through a digital service from end to end without assistance. This can mean that those who need the most support are often those who are least likely to get access to it.

Knowing what proportion of your service should be human is only one half of the problem; the other half comes in understanding what users need from this human contact.

The internet has changed what we need and expect from human contact in services. When your users have already understood what your service is and how to access it online, the people they interact with after this need to be far more expert than they were before, and crucially empowered to make decisions.

Regardless of the channel, there are certain principles that need to be followed when making sure your user can access the valuable skills of a human:

Be accessible when they're needed
Human decision-makers are often needed to make complex decisions, but sometimes those decisions are time critical. Getting in contact with a human needs to be fast.

Proportionally used
Incorporating human decision-makers into your service is vital, as we've seen. But it has to be used proportionally to the needs of your users and the service at hand. Too much contact and your service can disproportionately favour a small group of users over a wider selection, or prove to be unsustainable. Too few and your service is likely to not meet the most complex needs of users.

Empowered to make decisions
Possibly more important than the ability to be readily accessed is the ability of the people providing your service to make empowered decisions about the right thing to do in a given situation. This means removing organisational boundaries and ensuring that they are experts and multiskilled.

Consistent with the rest of the service
It's important that the way the humans providing your service work is consistent with the other channels your service is provided with, and with other humans also providing that service.

End note

It's hard to end a book like this.

If you've managed to read this book all the way through (well done!) you'll have seen some of the best and worst things that services can do to us. You'll be able to spot a good service when you see it, and know why a bad one is failing. Importantly, I hope that services aren't invisible to you, if they ever were before, and that you see them as tangible things that can and should be designed.

Following these principles will help make a service better for your organisation, your users and the world, but services are never really 'fixed'.

The world is always changing and, with it, our services need to evolve. Many of the services we use today are in such a poor state – not because we designed them badly in the first place, but because they have been neglected ever since.

A good service is not just easy to find, clear about its purpose, simple to use for the first time and consistent throughout. It doesn't just have to set a user's expectations, help them to do the thing they set out to do, in a way that's familiar for everyone who needs to use it.

Good services aren't just organisationally agnostic, seamless journeys that require the minimum possible steps to complete, in a way that responds to change in our lives quickly. And they don't just need to encourage the right behaviours of users and staff, clearly explain why decisions have been made by those staff or make it easy to get human assistance when we need it – all without causing dead ends that we can't get out of.

Good services need our constant, undivided attention. Because the biggest hurdle to designing a good service is to see it as a service in the first place.

Good luck.

BIS Publishers
Building Het Sieraad
Postjesweg 1
1057 DT Amsterdam
The Netherlands
T +31 (0)20 515 02 30
bis@bispublishers.com
www.bispublishers.com

ISBN 978 90 6369 543 9

Images: pages 16–17 Fred Morley / Hulton Archive /
Getty Images; pages 22–23 R. Jones / Hulton
Archive / Getty Images; pages 154–155 Jean-Michel
TURPIN / Gamma-Rapho / Getty Images

Copy-edited by Angus Montgomery and Claire
Sibbick Designed by Daly & Lyon

Thank you to everyone who has supported the
production of this book, particularly Chris Downs
for his wise and challenging advice.